Old Wives' Tales

FACT OR FOLKLORE?

Metro Books
122 Fifth Avenue
New York, NY 10011

ISBN-13: 978-1-4351-0755-7

Printed and bound in China

1 3 5 7 9 10 8 6 4 2

Old Wives' Tales

FACT OR FOLKLORE?

100 Popular Myths
Revealed and Explained

THOMAS CRAUGHWELL

METRO BOOKS
NEW YORK

CONTENTS

INTRODUCTION

*T*he basic fact about urban legends—those popular stories of stolen kidneys and alligators in sewers—is wonderfully simple: fundamentally, no urban legend is true. Old wives' tales, on the other hand, are more complicated. Some are obviously false. Others are based on a seed of truth. But there are some cases in which the old wives were right.

For example, generations have been nursed through colds and flu with a steaming bowl of chicken soup. In our skeptical age, most of us would regard this remedy as ineffective but harmless, a little comfort food for the patient. In fact, scientists across the globe agree that chicken soup really is good for cold and flu sufferers. As it simmers, the chicken releases into the broth the amino acid cysteine, which, just like the drug acetylcysteine prescribed for bronchitis and other respiratory ailments, reduces the buildup of mucus and helps the patient breathe easier.

Of course, there is more to old wives' tales than recipes from the Old Country. They are a mixed bag of sayings, folk customs, and superstitions that pass as common knowledge. Some old wives' tales stretch back to biblical times. In St. Matthew's gospel, for example, Jesus paraphrases the old saw, "Red sky at morning, sailors take warning. Red sky at night, sailor's delight."

The bulk of old wives' tales are concerned with the most important events in human life: marriage, sexual relations, pregnancy, childbirth, and raising children. The point of these old wives' tales is to avoid whatever is bad or harmful, encourage whatever is good, and give yourself an edge by being able to predict what is coming. Luck is another major preoccupation. Walking under a ladder invites bad luck. Not killing a ladybug invites good luck. But is there anything to these old folk beliefs? In many cases, yes. Walking under a ladder is not only unlucky, it can be fatal. Studies in the United States, the United Kingdom, and Sweden have found a near-epidemic of ladder-related accidents. As with stepping around ladders, leaving a ladybug unmolested is also sound advice. They are a gardener's friend, as they eat insects that attack tomatoes, cabbages, and broccoli.

Not all good luck/bad luck old wives' tales are rooted in basic safety precautions and rural wisdom. The unluckiness of Friday the 13th, for example, is based on two phobias: fear of Friday and fear of the number 13. It sounds laughable until you discover that every Friday the 13th, between $800 and $900 million in business is lost in the United States because people will not board airplanes, or make a major business decision, or dine out at a restaurant, or even show up for work.

One area in which the old wives drop the ball is weather. Since almost all old wives' tales date back to when the world was more rural than urban, more agricultural than industrial, you would think their observations about nature would be pretty reliable. But no. The old wives assure us that lightning never strikes the same place twice (tell that to the building manager of the Eiffel Tower). They say that tornadoes can't cross rivers (wrong again!). And their faith in a groundhog's ability to predict the coming of spring is touching, but nonetheless misguided.

The question for each old wives' tale is, "How true is it?" You'll find the short answer at the beginning of each tale, with a Veracity Meter designed exclusively for this book by the last twelve winners of the Nobel Prize for Physics, assisted by senior professors at the Massachusetts Institute of Technology. The result of this research is a scientifically precise measurement of the reliability of each old wives' tale. You believe us, right?

Inflated claims of rigorous scientific inquiry aside, a surprising number of old wives' tales are true—or at least partly true. Find out just how many of the old tales stand up to modern scrutiny.

LIGHTNING NEVER STRIKES THE SAME PLACE TWICE

HOW TRUE IS IT?
WAY OFF THE MARK.

small mountain of data tells us that lightning does in fact strike the same spot more than once. Some places are actually lightning magnets. Two of the world's most famous lightning rods are Paris's Eiffel Tower and New York City's Empire State Building: on average, both are struck by lightning 25 to 30 times every year. The Petronas Towers in Kuala Lumpur, Malaysia, and the Sears Tower in Chicago attract their share of electrical excitement, too.

One spectacular example of lightning striking the same place more than once, and in rapid succession, occurred among the tight cluster of skyscrapers that form the heart of downtown Oklahoma City, Oklahoma. These high-rise towers have been a favorite target for lightning bolts from the moment they were built. In one of Mother Nature's more dramatic demonstrations of just how offbase an old wives' tale can be, on May 29, 2001, these towers were struck repeatedly every 10 to 30 seconds.

And buildings aren't the only things that can attract lightning more than once. According to *The Guinness Book of World Records*, Roy Sullivan of Virginia holds the record for a human being who has suffered the most lightning strikes: between 1942 and 1977 he was hit seven times.

LIGHTNING FACTS

- A typical lightning bolt is about one inch wide.

- On average, a lightning bolt burns at about 27,000° Fahrenheit (about 15,000° Celsius). That's hotter than the surface of the sun (9,000° Fahrenheit or 5,000° Celsius).

- A lightning bolt generates 10–30 million volts of electricity. (A New York City subway train runs on 600 volts of electricity.)

- Lightning cranks out 25,000–30,000 amps of electrical current. (A household outlet produces about 15 amps.)

- On average, every commercial airliner in regular use takes two lightning strikes every year.

- Each second, between 50 and 100 lightning bolts strike the Earth.

- Lightning strikes most often in Central Africa, Florida, and Asia's Himalayas mountain range.

- It strikes least often in the Pacific islands, the North Pole, and the South Pole.

2

WE ARE TALLER THAN
OUR ANCESTORS

HOW TRUE IS IT?
THIS STORY ACTUALLY
MEASURES UP.

*V*isitors to historic homes often remark on how low the
ceilings are, and how small the beds. (Mind you, we're
talking the homes of ordinary folk, not Versailles.) Invariably,
either a tourist or the tour guide will assert that a couple
hundred years ago, people were shorter than they are today.
The most common reason offered is nutrition: thanks to
plentiful amounts of vitamin-rich food, we are giants when
compared to our ancestors. It seems to make sense, but
when it comes to old wives' tales it is best to be skeptical.
Nonetheless, Michael J. Dougherty, assistant director and
senior staff biologist at Biological Sciences Curriculum Study
in Colorado Springs, Colorado, says that "over the last 150
years the average height of people in industrialized nations has
increased approximately 10 centimeters (about four inches)."

Why the dramatic increase? Geneticists believe that better
nutrition, especially among children, has given our average height
a boost. And the evidence does seem to support this idea.
For example, from the first humans to the early 1800s, skeletal
remains show virtually no change in the height of the average
human. "Chronic underfeeding during childhood," Dougherty
explains, "permanently affects stature."

In other words, for thousands of years, most human children
were not getting enough nutritious food in order to grow
and develop. It is the chronic part that causes the trouble.
A temporary disruption in nutrition can be overcome later.
Dougherty cites the example of German children during World
War I and World War II: food was hard to come by in those

12

days, and children showed the effects of the food shortages by being slow to grow. After the wars were over, however, and food was plentiful again, the underdeveloped children of Germany recovered. According to Dougherty, "slow growth induced by temporary malnourishment can usually be reversed. Chronic underfeeding during childhood, however, permanently affects stature and other traits, including intelligence."

Does this mean humans will continue to grow ever taller until a seven-foot frame is the standard? The short answer is, "No." "The trend toward increasing height has largely leveled off," Dougherty says, "suggesting that there is an upper limit to height beyond which our genes are not equipped to take us, regardless of environmental improvements."

Thumb-Sucking Causes Buck Teeth

HOW TRUE IS IT?
TRUTH FROM THE MOUTHS
OF BABES.

Sucking on a thumb is hardwired into babies. Sonograms have shown unborn infants sucking their thumbs. Once a baby is born, sucking at its mother's breast or on a bottle becomes associated with warmth, security and the pleasantness of a full stomach. So in situations that make a little child nervous or uncomfortable, sucking on something can be reassuring.

Among toddlers aged 1 to 3, about 40 percent suck their thumb. About 33 percent of 3- to 5-year-olds continue the habit. At age 5 the number drops to about 25 percent. Thumb-sucking usually disappears in kindergarten or first grade, largely because of peer pressure. Now that we know that sucking a thumb is natural and eventually stops, the question remains, "Will it distort the shape of a child's mouth, create buck teeth, or otherwise require orthodontic work years later?"

The answer is a qualified yes. According to the American Academy of Pediatric Dentistry, long-term thumb-sucking can push the upper front teeth outward or otherwise distort the position of the teeth. A pacifier may be a solution, as these are soft and designed not to put pressure on the mouth. However, Jane Brody, health editor of the *New York Times*, says that in most cases, "as long as the habit is relinquished before the permanent teeth begin to emerge at about age 6, it rarely has a significant influence on mouth structures or tooth positions."

WAIT AN HOUR AFTER EATING BEFORE SWIMMING

HOW TRUE IS IT?
FEEL FREE TO EAT
HEARTILY, THEN TAKE
A DIP IN THE DRINK.

O f all the horror stories told to children, one of the most persistent is that any kid who does not wait an hour after eating before going into the water will develop a severe stomach cramp and drown.

It is true that in the United States drowning ranks as the highest cause of accidental death among infants and children. But these kids did not drown because they scorned the one-hour wait and raced from the picnic table straight to the swimming pool. Nonetheless, this old wives' tale endures. The precise date is fuzzy, but it was sometime in the 1930s old wives first adopted the formula "Lunch + Swimming = Death" as an article of faith.

Back in 1956, B.W. Gabrielsen, the swimming coach at the University of Georgia, published the book *Facts on Drowning Accidents*. In it he showed that jumping into the water after a meal led to fewer than 1 percent of all deaths by drowning— basically a statistical anomaly. In 1961, exercise physiologist Arthur Steinhaus concurred, publishing an article in the *Journal of Health, Physical Education, and Recreation* in which he dismissed any link between eating lunch and going swimming.

The digestion process breaks down food and liquid into small molecules of nutrients that can be absorbed by the cells and blood to nourish the body and provide energy. Swimming does not inhibit this natural process.

CRAVING SPICY FOOD MEANS YOU'RE HAVING A BOY

HOW TRUE IS IT?
THERE COULD BE A GRAIN
OF TRUTH TO THIS FOOD
FABLE.

According to the old wives, if a pregnant woman has a yen for Szechuan food, she should start thinking of boys' names. But if she can't stay away from the chocolatier, then a girl is on the way.

We have to admit that there is no evidence to support the spicy-or-sweet connection. But there has been one interesting study that finds a link between what an expectant mother eats and the sex of her unborn child. Professor Dimitrios Trichopoulos of Harvard University's School of Public Health followed the pregnancies of 250 American women. He found that women who gave birth to boys ate 8 percent more protein, 9 percent more carbohydrates, 11 percent more animal fats, and 15 percent more vegetable fats than women who gave birth to girls. Professor Trichopoulos proposes that a woman's body may be receiving signals from her unborn son, generated by the testosterone secreted from the fetal testicles, to eat more. The professor suggests that this could explain why newborn boys tend to weigh 3½ ounces (100 grams) more than newborn girls.

Professor Trichopoulos hasn't insisted that his study is conclusive and irrefutable, but it is interesting. Of course, there will always be scoffers. Elisabeth Gasparini, dietitian at Melbourne, Australia's Royal Women's Hospital, insists that the only way to find out the sex of an unborn baby is via ultrasound.

And while she was in debunking mode, Gasparini took a swipe at another food-based old wives' tale: that a pregnant mother should increase her food intake because she is eating for two. "Energy requirements for mothers-to-be are only slightly higher than normal," Gasparini insists, "and it's the quality of the food that's important, not the quantity."

WHAT TO EAT WHEN YOU'RE PREGNANT

- Milk, yogurt, hard pasteurized cheese such as cheddar, and fish such as salmon for calcium that will strengthen the baby's bones. But be careful! Do not eat unpasteurized blue cheeses or pasteurized soft cheeses while pregnant. These can carry a bacterium called Listeria monocytogenes, which can cause miscarriage.

- Red meat, legumes, nuts, wholegrain cereals, and green leafy vegetables for a healthy amount of iron in the infant's blood.

- Citrus fruits, berries, tomatoes, cabbage, broccoli, and cauliflower for Vitamin C to encourage the development of healthy teeth, gums, bones, and tissue.

TOADS GIVE YOU WARTS

HOW TRUE IS IT?
KISSING ONE IS JUST AS
LIKELY TO TURN IT INTO A
PRINCE AS GIVE YOU WARTS.

*T*he skin glands of toads secrete a slimy substance that can raise your blood pressure, give you hallucinations, and in some cases poison any dog or cat dumb enough to try to eat one. The skin of the cane toad, for example, is slick with a toxic compound called bufotenine. In Australia, scientists have found dead snakes that were killed so quickly by bufotenine that the cane toad the snake tried to eat was still in the snake's mouth, unswallowed. Some tribes in South America dip darts and arrows in cane toad toxin to kill their prey, and lick the secretion right off the cane toads to achieve a hallucinogenic ecstasy during religious ceremonies. But neither the toad's toxic gunk, nor the toad as a whole, will give you warts.

Warts are caused by papillomaviruses, a family of more than 70 viruses that afflict primates such as apes and humans. Toads and all other amphibians do not get papillomaviruses. In most cases when a papillomavirus makes contact with your skin, your body's immune system gets rid of it. If your immune system isn't operating very well, then the virus stays and you get warts.

Warts are one of the most common skin conditions on the planet. As you read this, one in every ten people has at least one wart. And 75 percent of the human population will have at least one wart in his or her lifetime. Most warts will go away on their own (after a year or so). If you'd rather not wait that long, a doctor can treat your warts with liquid nitrogen, which does not require a local anesthesia and eliminates the warts with minimal or no scarring.

Although toads cannot give you warts, raw meat and fish can. People who handle raw poultry, beef, and fish often develop what are known as "butcher's warts." Why working with raw meat or fish should produce warts is one of those mysteries that modern medicine still cannot explain.

WARTS ON YOUR SOLE

Among the most unpleasant warts are plantar warts that develop on the bottom of the feet. Because they are thick and the virus-infected area tends to reach deep into the foot tissue, plantar warts can sometimes make walking awkward and painful. Plantar warts can be removed surgically, but your walk will remain affected until the wound is fully healed. Depending on the size of the wart, healing could take weeks. If the plantar wart is caught early enough, when it is still very small, your doctor can remove it with liquid nitrogen. Once the plantar wart is larger than half an inch (1 centimeter) in diameter, however, it's too big for a liquid nitrogen treatment. At that point, surgery is the only option.

NUMBER EIGHT IS LUCKY IN CHINA

HOW TRUE IS IT?
IT HARDLY MATTERS.

*D*oing everything to ensure good luck and avoid bad luck can be a full-time occupation in China—and not just among old wives. Even young computer geeks and international business moguls worry about such things. Consider the number 8: in Chinese it is pronounced "ba," which is close to the Mandarin and Cantonese word "*fa*," which means "to prosper." As a result, 8 is the most auspicious and desirable of lucky numbers in Chinese culture. How desirable? In August 2003, executives of Sichuan Airlines paid 2.33 million yuan (in U.S. dollars that's $288,000) in a special auction to secure 8888-8888 as the company's 24-hour customer-service hotline. If one eight is good, eight eights all in a row must be exceptional. It is the equivalent of hitting the good-luck jackpot. Xing Bing, a spokesperson for Sichuan Airlines, assured a reporter from the Associated Press, "Everyone at the company believes the number was worth the price we paid."

Chinese immigrants to the United States have brought their faith in lucky number eight with them. Realtors in California's San Gabriel Valley have learned that among Chinese house buyers, an eight in the address is perceived as value-added. And just like the executives of Sichuan Airlines, the Chinese immigrants will pay a premium for phone numbers, fax numbers, automobile license plates, and bank account numbers that carry a lot of eights. Flip through the Chinese Yellow Pages for San Gabriel Valley, and the number eight is everywhere.

On the flip side, the numbers 4 and 14 are notoriously unlucky. It would be hard to find a high-rise in Beijing that lists a fourth or fourteenth floor in its directory.

A Westerner who writes a regular column on life in China for the website www.pekingduck.org found out why most Chinese prefer to keep 4 and 14 at arm's length. After he had been assigned a new phone number that included the digits 14114, a friend explained to him that in Chinese "one" sounds like the verb "want" and "four" sounds like the word "die." To any Chinese calling him, the expatriate's new phone number read, "I want to die, I want, I want to die."

ELEPHANTS ARE AFRAID OF MICE

HOW TRUE IS IT?
ONLY A TINY BIT TRUE.

*T*here's a scene in the Walt Disney cartoon *Dumbo* in which some elephants are being mean to the little guy. A mouse marches in among the herd to stand up for Dumbo. Naturally, all the elephants panic in comically Disneyesque kinds of ways.

Disney didn't invent the story that elephants are afraid of mice; it only capitalized on something everybody knows to be true. But are the old wives right? Can a tiny mouse really panic a pachyderm? It depends on the circumstances.

Generally speaking, elephants aren't afraid of anything. As the biggest land animal in the world, they have no predators except man. Since they are vegetarians with no need to stalk their prey, keen eyesight is not essential. In fact, they do not see very well, a characteristic compounded by the fact that their eyes are on the sides of their head rather than the front. Consequently, if something tiny should dart around an elephant's feet, the creature is spooked and will stomp erratically to get away from, or maybe trample, whatever is down there. This rarely occurs in the wild, but in zoos and circuses it's not unusual for a mouse to get into an elephant's enclosure. The captive elephant's response to the rodent is the likely source of this myth.

Elephants do have one fear that they share with humans: both species are frightened when they encounter the bones of their own kind.

READING IN DIM LIGHT RUINS YOUR EYES

HOW TRUE IS IT?
THIS TALE IS NONE
TOO BRIGHT.

*T*urning the lights down low may create atmosphere, but it drives old wives to distraction. "Turn on more lights!" they cry. "Do you want to go blind?"

At first, you might think that the old wives are right. Trying to read in dim light strains the eyes. Eyestrain could lead to eye damage. Read in the semi-dark often enough, and perhaps you will eventually go blind. Such reasoning seems unassailable, but before you fire up every lamp in the house, let's ask an expert.

Dr. Eugene Folk is quoted in *Eye Facts*, a publication of the Eye Center of the University of Illinois at Chicago College of Medicine, as saying, "Although reading in dim light is unwise because it may cause your eyes to feel tired or uncomfortable, it can't hurt your eyes." Similarly, "reading small print or reading extensively cannot cause damage to the eyes," he says. "This is true even for people who already have poor vision."

The American Academy of Ophthalmology (AAO) backs this up. "You can't wear out your eyes by using them," it says. The only issue in regard to reading in dim light is "good light makes reading easier and prevents eye fatigue." But what about spending hours working on a computer? Surely that causes eye damage. Once again, the AAO is reassuring. "Working on computers will not harm your eyes." The AAO recommends taking regular breaks from the computer. Just looking away from the screen at an object across the room will help.

IT'S BAD LUCK TO CHANGE A BOAT'S NAME

HOW TRUE IS IT?
IT DOESN'T HOLD WATER.

No less an authority than Robert Louis Stevenson defended the practice of never changing a boat's name. In his 1881 novel *Treasure Island*, he tells of a seaman who tempted fate by changing the names of his ships and ended up "hanged like a dog." According to folklore, changing a boat's name is like changing a person's name—it's bad form, plain and simple. Furthermore, just as a child receives its name at baptism, the ship receives its name in a christening ceremony. The way the old seadogs see it, to dispense with one name and adopt another is to tempt Providence.

In our own day, less orthodox types also warn against changing a boat's name. Numerologists claim that each letter of a name possesses a numerical equivalent with a unique energy. These energies endow the boat with a mystical guardian force. To change the name would scramble the boat's energy and cause no end of trouble to the boat and its owner.

Boating writer John Vigor has come up with a Boat Denaming Ceremony in which the boat owner asks permission of Neptune, god of the sea, and Aeolus, god of the winds, before renaming the boat. That said, the author of an article on the protocol for renaming a boat admits that a boating friend of his owned 24 yachts and renamed each one. This plucky yachtsman was never beset by pirates, nor shipwrecked, nor attacked by a vengeful white whale.

CURVY WOMEN WERE BUILT FOR CHILD-BEARING

HOW TRUE IS IT?
MOTHER NATURE KNEW
WHAT SHE WAS DOING.

*T*hroughout history old wives have assured curvaceous women, "You have the hips for child-bearing." It's meant as a compliment. Although these days, when undernourished actresses and pop stars have the look women are supposed to want, it's not likely to win an old wife any friends.

A 2004 article in Melbourne, Australia's *Herald Sun* reported that scientists in the United States have found that shapely women really are designed to make babies. The data was based on a study of 119 women. Over several months, the researchers collected daily saliva samples from the women and recorded the levels of oestradiol and progesterone, two hormones that are essential to fertility. At the women's most fertile times of the month, the fertility hormone level of curvaceous women was 37 percent higher than that of their slender sisters.

The big-hip syndrome also has reverberations among men. Who are the classic sex goddesses? Marilyn Monroe, Sophia Loren, Mae West, Jayne Mansfield. And these days, Jennifer Lopez. All voluptuous females who fit perfectly the requirements of this latest study. Why are they the fantasy objects of so many men? The researchers suggest that it's a subconscious thing that has evolved over thousands of years: trial and error has taught men to be drawn to women who are most likely to reproduce. In other words, women with the hips for child-bearing.

A FULL MOON CAUSES STRANGE BEHAVIOR

HOW TRUE IS IT?
THIS ONE MIGHT BE
FULL OF IT.

*T*he terms "loony" and "lunatic" both come from the Latin word *luna*, which means, "the moon." As old wives' tales go, belief in the link between oddball behavior and a full moon is extremely ancient. And the anecdotal evidence to back up the old wives is extensive.

In 2000, doctors at England's Bradford Royal Infirmary reported that during the three days on and around the full moon, they treated twice as many patients for animal bites, which suggested to them that the moon might be getting the animals worked up. In terms of human mayhem, a 1987 survey reported that 80 percent of emergency room nurses and 64 percent of emergency room doctors believed they saw more murder victims during a full moon than on other days of the month.

The anecdotal evidence doesn't end there. The notorious 1970s New York City serial killer, David Berkowitz ("Son of Sam") killed five of his eight victims during a full moon. Serial killer Charles Hyde, who terrified England in the 1880s, did most of his murdering under a full moon. (By the way, the Hyde case was the inspiration for Robert Louis Stevenson's novel, *Dr. Jekyll and Mr. Hyde.*) Meanwhile, the *British Medical Journal* found links between the full moon and a sharp increase in criminal behavior, as well as drunkenness, drug overdoses, and even traffic accidents.

In 2002 *The San Francisco Chronicle* conducted its own study to see if there was any link between a full moon and the number of murders committed in the city between 1997 and 2001.

The reporters found that in 1997 there were nine full-moon murders; seven in 1998; seven in 1999; nine in 2000; and 14 in 2001. On the surface, the numbers look impressive—until you realize that the reporters failed to compare the number of murders on full-moon nights against the number of murders committed on nights when the moon was not full. Alas, sloppy studies only reinforce the full-moon myth.

Another example: in the 1970s, University of Miami psychologist Arthur Lieber surveyed 15 years of data from the Dade County Police Department's homicide files and concluded that murders followed the phases of the moon, with the number of homicides reaching their peak at the full moon. But Lieber's "data" didn't stand up under examination. An astronomer, Nicholas Sanduleak, double-checked Lieber's figures and found no correlation between the full moon and an increase in homicides. It didn't help Lieber's case that, to account for the rise and fall of homicides, he offered the novel and decidedly unscientific suggestion that because the human body is mostly water and the moon has influence on the tides, the pull of a full moon affects people in unpredictable ways.

San Francisco's coroner, Dr. Boyd Stephens, has a different theory. A night with a full moon is attractive and exciting. On such a night, Dr. Stephens says, "People tend to go outdoors, they tend to drink, they tend to party, and that's when they get in trouble." It appears, then, that in the case of the truth or falsehood of this old wives' tale, the jury is still out—but the anecdotal evidence urges caution.

GROUNDHOGS CAN PREDICT THE END OF WINTER

HOW TRUE IS IT?
IT DEPENDS ON WHICH GROUNDHOG YOU'RE WATCHING.

*T*hanks to the 1993 romantic comedy *Groundhog Day*, starring Bill Murray and Andie MacDowell, many of us are familiar with Punxsutawney, Pennsylvania. At least since 1887, this little town has been relying on its famous groundhog, Phil, to predict whether winter is over or if we're in for another six weeks of nasty weather.

It's all very scientific, of course. On February 2, just about halfway between the winter solstice and the spring equinox, all eyes turn to a groundhog burrow. If the groundhog comes out and sees his shadow, he gets frightened, scampers back inside, and winter drags on for another six weeks. If the groundhog does not see his shadow, however, he goes on his merry way and we can look forward to an early spring.

The people of Punxsutawney insist that their groundhog, Punxsutawney Phil, is the one and only entirely reliable prognosticator of the coming of spring. Certainly the movie has gone a long way to making Punxsutawney Phil the world's most famous groundhog. It has transformed the town's celebration of Groundhog Day from a modest local event into a major celebration with crowds of visitors cramming into Punxsutawney to witness Phil's remarkable feat of forecasting.

The Punxsutawneyians claim that Phil's predictions are 100 percent accurate. A quick look at the numbers, however, makes one wonder if perhaps Phil's stats haven't been massaged by Punxsutawney's Visitors and Conventions Bureau. In fact, Phil's accuracy rate hovers at or below the 39 percent mark.

If Vegas were giving Groundhog Day odds, the smart money would not be on Phil.

It may be heresy—or at least treason—but other localities tout their own groundhogs. Shubenacadie Sam, who makes his home in Nova Scotia's Shubenacadie Wildlife Park, claims to be Canada's first prognosticating groundhog. In 1979, on what must have been a slow day for legislation, the Ohio General Assembly declared Buckeye Chuck of Marion, Ohio, the official State Groundhog. Meanwhile in Louisiana, where nothing is what you would expect it to be, the state groundhog is actually a crawfish named Claude.

Giving Punxsutawney Phil a serious run for his money is New York City's Staten Island Chuck, who has rendered predictions that Staten Islanders insist are 84 percent accurate! Chuck's handlers would also like to offer you the Brooklyn Bridge at a very reasonable price…

IF YOU CROSS YOUR EYES, THEY WILL STAY THAT WAY

HOW TRUE IS IT?
LOOK ASKANCE AT THIS ONE.

Old wives take particular delight in warning children that an action that appears to be completely innocent will result in dire, lifelong consequences. Crossing your eyes as a means of mindless entertainment is one of them. Crossed eyes (doctors call it strabismus) are serious business. But you cannot cause the condition by playing at having it. There is no tiny switch behind your eyeballs waiting to lock into place because you were dumb enough to cross your eyes.

Let's look at the real causes of crossed eyes. In most cases, a kid inherits the condition from his or her parents. Loss of vision in one eye can cause strabismus. So can any of a host of eye diseases. There are also cases in which the eye muscles are fine, but the coordination mechanism for the two eyes doesn't work properly.

Children do not outgrow strabismus, but they can be treated. Eyeglasses will often do the trick—and they have been prescribed, with good results, for babies as young as six months. If one eye turns outward, or if the eyes are not aligned properly (meaning one eye is higher than the other), then surgery is required. And it is the eye muscles that are operated on, not the eyes themselves. In almost all cases, one operation is all it takes to correct the problem.

RED SKY IN THE MORNING FORECASTS A STORM

HOW TRUE IS IT?
SEAFARING FOLKLORE
WORTH HEEDING.

*E*ven people who've never owned a boat know the adage, "Red sky at morning, sailors take warning. Red sky at night, sailor's delight." But the proverb is not limited to sailors. In the bible Christ says, "When it is evening, you say, 'It will be fair weather for the sky is red.' And in the morning, 'Today there will be a storm, for the sky is red and lowering'" (Matthew 16, 2–3).

At the risk of sounding like Doubting Thomas, we'd still like some data before we accept that the maxim is true. And it is! According to Joe Sienkiewicz, chief of the Ocean Applications Branch and a science and operations officer with the National Weather Service's Ocean Prediction Center, the saying applies to Earth's mid-latitudes where weather systems—clear or stormy—move from west to east. When the morning sun rises on an approaching storm, it casts its light on "the approaching mid- and high-level clouds to create a red sky in the morning."

On the other hand, Sienkiewicz explains, if the sun sets in the evening "as a weather system exits and high pressure is building, then the departing clouds would be illuminated. This would create a red sky at night with fair weather to follow." So the saying is true, as long as the weather is moving in its usual west-to-east pattern. Once in a great while, however, a weather system will travel from south to north, and in that case, the "red sky" old wives' tale does not apply.

Opals are Unlucky Unless it is Your Birthstone

How True Is It?
WEAR THEM WITHOUT FEAR.

At least 1,000 years ago old wives had convinced even educated people that the opal was an unlucky stone. In the 11th century, Bishop Marbode of Rennes damned opals as "the guardian of the thievish race." He was alluding to a superstition that an opal rendered the wearer invisible —which made the stone very popular among thieves, burglars, and even spies.

Not everyone was so negative about opals. The ancient Greeks thought the stone gave the wearer the ability to tell the future. The stone's myriad colors reminded the ancient Romans of a rainbow, so they carried it as a talisman that would bring them good luck. And the Arabs believed the opal must have fallen from heaven—it was their way of accounting for its beauty.

Still, the bad reputation that the opal acquired in the Middle Ages hung on in the modern era. During the 19th century, many people believed that only those individuals born in October could safely wear the opal, their month's birthstone. Although most of us probably do not worry about donning the fiery gem even if we do not have October birthdays, many contemporary jewelers take care to dispute any lingering fears we may still have about purchasing a piece of opal jewelry.

Australians have been working hard to dispel the slur against the opal. They like to tell the story of Harry Brukarz, a Sydney jeweler who specialized in opals. Throughout the 1940s and 1950s, Brukarz won lottery after lottery. He attributed his extraordinary luck to his opals.

The opal has been very, very good to Australia. Some of the most magnificent opals in the world have been found there, including the 180-carat "Aurora Australis," the world's most valuable black opal, discovered in 1938 at Lightning Ridge. In 2005 this stone was appraised for AUD$1 million. Leaving "Aurora Australis" in the dust is "Olympic Australis," the largest gem opal ever found. In 1956 a miner working the famous opal field in Coober Pedy, South Australia, found the stone 30 feet (9 meters) down. It weighs 17,000 carats and was valued in 2005 at AUD$2.5 million. The gem is of such extraordinary purity that jewelers believe at least 7,000 carats could be cut from it. Since it is such a unique piece, however, it will remain intact.

Naturally, these fabulous opals have passed through the hands of countless individuals who were not born in October. Yet no epidemic of tragedies has been reported.

COFFEE STUNTS CHILDREN'S GROWTH

HOW TRUE IS IT?
THERE'S SOME TRUTH
HERE—BUT MOST KIDS
DON'T LIKE COFFEE
ANYWAY!

Concerned grandparents who would never dream of giving their grandchildren coffee because it will stunt the kids' growth will cheerfully pass around cans of soft drinks. There is a factual disconnect going on here, because the coffee and virtually all soft drinks are laden with caffeine.

A high intake of caffeine does cause the body to lose the calcium and potassium it needs in order for bone to grow. One study found that caffeine decreases bone-mineral density in teenage girls. The same study concluded, however, that the ill effects of caffeine can be offset by drinking just one glass of milk per day. In other words, unless a kid is knocking back double shots of espresso all day long, there's not much to worry about. However, the diuretic effects of caffeine in soft drinks may cause problems—it causes thirsty kids to become even more dehydrated. The best option is to drink water or fruit or vegetable juices rather than soft drinks.

Dr. Manfred Kroger, professor of food science at Pennsylvania State University, has explained that caffeine is more of an issue for kids than for adults because a child's body is smaller and it tends to retain caffeine in its system longer than is the case with adults. Consequently, Dr. Kroger recommends that kids consume no more than 100 milligrams of caffeine a day. That translates to about two cans of soda, one shot of espresso, or one cappuccino.

Boys Who Drink Coffee Will Be Beardless

How True Is It?
ONLY IF THEY SHAVE.

Old wives in Turkey fear that young boys who drink coffee will never grow a beard. Could there be a link between caffeine and testosterone? Professor Peter Elsner and his team at Jena University in Germany found that there is indeed a link—but not in the way the old wives fear. Caffeine products, the researchers found, can actually stop men from going bald.

Guys with high testosterone levels tend to have a lot of body and facial hair. It's a matter of genetics. Some families have buckets of the 5-alpha reductase enzyme, which encourages testosterone to produce a heavy beard and a jungle of hair on a man's chest, belly, and back. There is a downside to all this masculinity: what the 5-alpha reductase enzyme giveth, the 5-alpha reductase enzyme also taketh away. Or to put it in plain English, hairy-chested he-men tend to go bald.

The trick to stimulating hair growth is not drinking coffee—you'd have to drink 60 to 80 cups per day before there was enough caffeine in your system to reach the roots of your hair. Instead, you must rub the caffeine extract right on the place where you want the hair to grow. Professor Elsner's study found that the caffeine treatment, on average, increased hair growth by 46 percent and extended the life cycle of the hair by 37 percent. If baldness runs in your family, Professor Elsner suggests you take action now by massaging a caffeine solution into your scalp so your hair won't fall out later.

MAGNETS HEAL FASTER THAN CONVENTIONAL MEDICINE

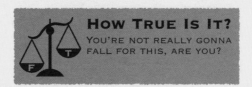

HOW TRUE IS IT?
YOU'RE NOT REALLY GONNA
FALL FOR THIS, ARE YOU?

Over the last 500 years various people have touted the "miraculous" healing properties of the humble magnet. The first was the 16th-century alchemist/physician Paracelsus, who saw how a magnet could draw to itself metal objects that were some distance away and concluded (wrongly) that anything that powerful must have powerful healing properties.

100 years later, English charlatan Dr. Robert Fludd claimed he could cure any ailment with his magnets, provided the patient stayed in the "boreal position" (with his head pointing north and his feet pointing south) while the magnets worked their magic.

The most famous proponent of magnetism was Franz Mesmer (whose name gave us the word "mesmerize"). He came from Vienna to Paris in 1778, where he "healed" people by having them sit around a vat of what he described as "magnetized water" while holding iron rods in their hands. King Louis XVI asked Antoine Lavoissier, the founder of modern chemistry, and Benjamin Franklin, who was in Paris at the time as the ambassador for the American colonies, to look into Mesmer's methods. They found that the only power Mesmer and his magnets exerted was the power of suggestion.

In the late 1990s, magnets became fashionable again, this time among professional athletes. Miami Dolphins quarterback Dan Marino reportedly used magnets to speed up healing a broken ankle. Yankee center fielder Bernie Williams used them for an injured hamstring, while pro golfer Bob Murphy admitted to strapping magnets to his body as an antidote to growing old.

In a "Health Report" segment broadcast on *ABC World News Tonight* in August, 1997, telejournalist Juju Chang reported that healing magnets had become a multimillion-dollar business. The report featured a series of therapeutic magnet experts. One claimed that magnetism can alter human tissue. Another said that "every human cell has a positive and a negative side to it." A third claimed that magnets draw more blood to an injured area, and that magnets can do this because blood contains iron.

In *Voodoo Science: The Road from Foolishness to Fraud*, physicist Robert L. Park tackled the claims regarding the health benefits of magnets. First, it is a biological impossibility for magnets to alter tissue. Second, human cells do not have positive and negative sides. Third, magnets do not draw blood to an afflicted area of the body. You can test this assertion at home. Apply a heating pad to any part of your body. That area becomes flushed because the blood is drawn to the area to cool it down. Now strap a magnet to a part of your body. Nothing happens. Why? Because the iron in blood are in a chemical state; they aren't microscopic splinters of metal floating around in your bloodstream that can be drawn by a magnet.

Finally, Park tested the strength of the magnets in a therapeutic magnet kit. He found they could hold nine sheets of ordinary paper to the side of his steel file cabinet. When Park added a tenth sheet, however, the magnet's force couldn't penetrate the paper and everything fell to the floor. Ten sheets of paper is just 1 millimeter thick. Even if magnets worked, they would barely penetrate the skin, which ranges in thickness from .05 millimeter on the eyelid to 4 millimeters on the soles of the feet. So it is impossible that the force of the magnets could reach down into torn muscle or broken bones.

YOU'RE CARRYING A GIRL IF YOUR FACE IS PUFFY

HOW TRUE IS IT?
THERE'S A BLUSH OF
TRUTH TO THIS ONE.

*A*ccording to the old wives, an unborn girl saps her mother's good looks—hence the puffy face, straggly hair, and extra weight around the pregnant woman's hips. There may be something to this old wives' tale, but if so, it is not an example of *in utero* family rivalry. Some scientists have speculated that when a woman is carrying a girl, her body produces more estrogen. It is the estrogen that packs more fat on the hips. As for the stringy hair and puffy face, the scientists cannot come to any conclusions.

If science is studying possible links between thin, lifeless hair and the gender of an unborn child, it might as well branch out into other unconventional methods of predicting a baby's sex. Psychologist Janet DiPietro, who studies fetal development at the Johns Hopkins School of Public Health in Baltimore, has conducted a study of the dreams of 104 pregnant mothers, all of whom had more than 12 years of formal schooling. About 75 percent of the time, women who dreamed they would have a boy did indeed give birth to a boy, and women who dreamed they would have a girl gave birth to a girl. Interestingly, the dreams of pregnant women with less schooling were an accurate predictor only 43 percent of the time—which places their dreams solidly in the coin-toss territory.

IT'S BAD LUCK TO KILL A BEE

HOW TRUE IS IT?
UNLESS IT'S STINGING YOU,
LEAVE IT BE.

You won't be forever accursed with bad luck by the insect gods if you swat a bee, but considering all the benefits a bee provides, it really is wiser to leave the little creature alone.

First, bees produce honey. For centuries before mankind figured out how to process cane sugar, honey was the world's primary sweetener. Although the market for honey has shrunk, it is still delicious. Then there is the purely practical consideration: without pollination the world would be a wasteland. And the most industrious of nature's pollinators is the bee. Gardeners learned long ago that keeping a beehive or two in the backyard improved their harvest of fruits, vegetables, and flowers.

At San Francisco University Dr. Keith Slessor, a chemist, and Dr. Mark Winston, an entomologist, developed a synthetic pheromone that mimics the substance secreted by a queen bee to attract worker bees. The substance encourages worker bees to collect more pollen. Commercial fruit growers found that when they sprayed the synthetic bee pheromone on their trees and plants during the flowering season, they saw a net profit increase of $1,400 per hectare for pears, $1,270 for highbush blueberries, and up to $6,340 per hectare for cranberries.

If you aren't inclined to keep a beehive, you can still attract bees to your garden. Plant colorful flowers, and sow sweet-smelling herbs such as basil. Bees find both irresistible.

KILL A COBRA AND ITS MATE WILL COME AFTER YOU

HOW TRUE IS IT?
DON'T BE HISS-TERICAL.

In India the old wives say that if you kill a cobra, make sure you dispose of the body far from your home. Otherwise the mate will see your reflection locked in the dead cobra's eyes and come looking for you.

The idea that some animals have human intelligence and will come after us shows up in folklore across the world. It's even made its way in classic literature (Herman Melville's novel of a vengeful white whale, *Moby Dick*) and blockbuster movies (Steven Spielberg's film of a giant man-stalking shark, *Jaws*). It is true that some wild animals are man-hunters: grizzly bears and tigers have been known to go after humans who invade their habitats. Cobras, however, do not hunt people. And that's just the first thing that's off-base about this particular old wives' tale.

Next there is the question of the picture in the dead cobra's eyes. Eyes are not cameras. They do not store images of what they've seen—not even the picture of the person who killed the eyes' owner. Besides, a cobra does not use its eyes to hunt; it uses its sense of smell, which is concentrated not in the nostrils but in the cobra's long tongue. By flicking out its tongue, the cobra gets a sense of what is in the neighborhood.

Then there is the revenge question. If you did something to make a cobra feel endangered, it would retaliate by trying to bite you. But we're talking about a direct cause-and-effect situation. Let's say you take a swing at a cobra with a stick. You miss. It strikes out at you. It misses. You run back to the house; the cobra slinks off into the grass. Back in its lair the cobra is not nursing a grudge, waiting for the day when it can finally nail you and pump 350 milligrams of venom into your bloodstream.

Finally, we come to the issue of the cobra's mating habits. Unlike beavers, cobras do not mate for life. During mating season male cobras compete for a female. Once a male and female have paired up, the female makes a nest in which she lays between 30 and 50 eggs. During the three months it takes for the eggs to hatch, the male stays close to the nest, ready to kill any predator that comes near. Once the cobra hatchlings emerge, however, the male cobra slithers away. Cobras possess no sense of family loyalty.

THROW RICE AT A WEDDING
FOR GOOD LUCK

HOW TRUE IS IT?

THE ONLY THING IT BRINGS
THEM IS GRAINS OF RICE IN
UNCOMFORTABLE PLACES.

*T*he custom of showering newlyweds with grain is ancient. More than 2,000 years ago, the Romans tossed grains of wheat at the bride and groom, wheat being a symbol of fertility and prosperity. A Roman bride reinforced the custom by wearing a garland of wheat in her hair, and carrying a small sheaf of wheat as a bridal bouquet. The Romans regarded the grains of wheat that bounced off the bride as especially lucky: unmarried girls scrambled to collect these grains to ensure that they would be the next to marry.

Perhaps because of the influence of the Roman Empire, the tradition of throwing wheat at a wedding became widespread across ancient Europe and survived through the Middle Ages. In the 16th century, during the reign of Queen Elizabeth I, the custom experienced an odd metamorphosis. Instead of showering wheat on the happy couple, wedding guests tossed tiny cakes at them. No one knows why the tradition changed. But we can guess why the cake-tossing tradition didn't last long. It had to be a messy affair.

During the 17th century, in place of throwing little cakes, the wedding guests were invited to eat a share of one large cake. This was undeniably tidier. Yet the impulse to sling something at a bride and groom is deeply rooted in the human race. And so by the 18th century the old tradition was revived with rice— cheap, readily available, and already bridal-white by nature.

No doubt some of our readers are repulsed by the thought of tossing uncooked white rice outdoors. "What about the birds?"

they wail. At least since the 1990s a new old wives' tale has attached itself to this venerable wedding custom. According to this latest myth, the stomachs of wild birds cannot digest raw white rice. The grains puff up in the bird's stomach until the tiny creature explodes.

Who would fall for such nonsense? Millions of people—especially after the advice columnist Ann Landers urged her readers in 1996 to think about our feathered friends. "Please encourage the guests to throw rose petals instead of rice," she said. "Rice is not good for the birds."

"This silly myth pops up periodically, and it is absolutely unfounded," said Mary Jo Cheesman of the USA Rice Federation. Given Ms. Cheesman's association with the USA Rice Federation, she may not be an entirely unbiased source. Nonetheless, she has some good arguments. She points out that wild birds feed in rice fields all the time. If raw rice eaten off the stalk doesn't make them blow up, why would raw rice that they pick up off the church steps do so?

Ornithologists dismiss the myth, too. Biologist Ned Johnson who lectures at the University of California at Berkeley on the care and feeding of birds, says "There is no reason why birds, including small songbirds, can't eat rice."

So at the next wedding you attend, let the rice fly.

Fear Can Turn Hair White Overnight

How True Is It?
THIS HAIR-RAISING MYTH
HAS SOME TRUTH IN IT.

*I*t's said that the night before she went to the guillotine, Marie Antoinette was so terrified that between dusk and dawn her hair turned white. This old wives' tale about the power of fear or anxiety to whiten hair has enjoyed wide circulation for centuries. Marie Antoinette herself believed it. After she and the rest of the royal family failed to escape from France, she sent a lock of hair to her friend, the Princesse de Lamballe, with a note saying, "Unhappiness turned it white."

The queen's biographer, Antonia Fraser, tells us that Marie Antoinette's hair had been going white (or at least gray) for years. Before the French Revolution, when she had hairdressers powdering, pomading, and coloring her hair, the queen probably would not have noticed the gray. Once her troubles began and the hairdressers were no longer around to tend the royal coiffure, the white hairs would have become noticeable. In keeping with the myth, the queen would have blamed her white hair on her sorrows, not her lack of access to hair dyes.

There is another possibility: a condition called diffuse alopecia areata can cause sudden loss of dark or pigmented hair, leaving the white or gray hairs behind. Doctors haven't been able to pinpoint what biological conditions set off alopecia, but there is some evidence that shock or stress contributes to it. This gives the impression that someone's hair has "turned white overnight."

To Bring Good Luck, Knock on Wood

How True Is It?
IT DOESN'T HAVE A PRAYER.

*T*he ancient Celts were tree people: they regarded the oak, the ash, the holly, and the hawthorn as especially sacred, but they also believed that every tree had a protective spirit that could do mankind good. If 2,000 years ago a Celtic chieftain announced to his tribe, "Tomorrow we're going to vanquish the Romans!" he would knock on a tree, a door beam, or any other piece of wood so that the guardian spirit would emerge to make what the chieftain hoped for come true and drive away any evil spirits who might want to thwart the chief's plans. The tradition of knocking on wood was so pervasive in the Celtic world that even after the Celts were converted to Christianity they still kept up this custom. The Church "baptized" it, as it were, by suggesting that knocking on wood was a harmless commemoration of the True Cross.

A variation on this theme developed in Ireland. When someone in Ireland has experienced a bit of good luck, the tradition is to knock on wood to thank the little people who dwell there and made it all possible.

There are no statistics about the efficacy of knocking on wood. But we're willing to go out on a limb and state that it is unlikely that every tree, let alone every scrap of lumber, harbors a dryad waiting to do good in the world. By the way, "knock on wood" is the American version. In the British Isles they say "touch wood."

WHY GOLF COURSES HAVE EIGHTEEN HOLES

HOW TRUE IS IT?
TOTALLY OFF THE FAIRWAY.

*E*verybody knows that the Scots love golf, and the Scots love Scotch. Isn't it natural, then, that when designing the world's first golf course they would have based the number of holes on the number of shots contained in a standard-size bottle of Scotch whiskey?

The short answer is, "No." Think about it: who could possibly walk across the fairway, let alone hit a little white ball, with 18 shots of straight whiskey in his system? But logical explanations aside, there is also a historical one.

Although there has been a form of golf around at least since the days of the Romans, the number of holes on early golf courses differed vastly, even in Scotland. Scotland's Leith Links, for example, had only five holes, while the Montrose Links had 25. Golfers have been playing at the internationally famous St. Andrews course—a narrow strip of land along the seashore—since the 15th century. The course originally had 11 holes that began virtually at the clubhouse door and stretched to the end of the property. You played the 11 holes out, then turned around and played the same holes back to the clubhouse. That made for a 22-hole game at St. Andrews. Then, in 1764, the "Captain and Gentlemen Golfers," as the members of the St. Andrews club called themselves, decided that their first four holes were too short. They ordered them to be consolidated into just two holes, thereby transforming St. Andrews into an 18-hole golf course.

Standardization came slowly to golf. By 1882, two of the most prestigious golf clubs in the world—Prestwick and Muirfields—had 18-hole courses, which went a long way to making 18 holes the norm. Then, in 1897, The Royal and Ancient Golf Club of St. Andrews was given authority to set the rules for golf. If ever there was an opportunity to make 18 holes official, this was it. Still, St. Andrews held back. It was not until 1950 that it was set down in the Rules of Golf that 18 holes was designated as a "stipulated round."

IF THE LABOR IS DIFFICULT, YOU'RE HAVING A BOY

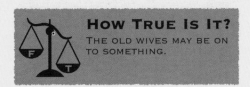

HOW TRUE IS IT?
THE OLD WIVES MAY BE ON TO SOMETHING.

*I*n Ireland, old wives who double as midwives say that a difficult delivery means that a boy is coming. So between 1997 and 2000, researchers conducted a study at the National Maternity Hospital in Dublin, Ireland. They based their study on 4,070 boys and 4,005 girls born to first-time mothers. The results surprised everyone (except the old wives).

A new mother had a 76 percent chance—or better—of an easy delivery if she was carrying a girl. Her chances dipped to 71 percent if she was carrying a boy. Equipment such as forceps were necessary in the delivery of 23 percent of boy newborns, but only 18 percent of girl newborns. Furthermore, 6 percent of the boys delivered required a Caesarean section, while just a shade over 4 percent of the girls required one.

While the study produced intriguing numbers, researchers have not been able to suggest a cause. There is supporting data that newborn boys have larger heads than newborn girls, which could prolong labor and require Caesarean sections. But baby boys are also more likely to experience fetal distress, which has nothing to do with head size. So, in spite of the Irish study, the reason for the correlation between gender and a difficult delivery remains a mystery.

A Cricket in the House is Good Luck

HOW TRUE IS IT?
ONLY IF YOU CONSIDER
INSECT INFESTATIONS
GOOD FORTUNE.

*I*n almost every part of the world a cricket in the house is considered good luck. In China, a whole "cricket culture" developed some 2,000 years ago. The Chinese valued large families with many children. Since crickets lay hundreds of eggs, they were considered models of fruitfulness and prosperity. In some parts of China, it was traditional to wish newlyweds as many children as a cricket. During the Tang Dynasty (500 B.C.– 618 A.D.) it became the custom to keep a cricket in a beautiful box or cage so people could enjoy the cricket's music wherever they went. This custom spread to Japan and even to Europe.

Unlike other varieties such as locusts, which devour crops, and mole crickets, which ruin plants and lawns by chewing through the roots, the house cricket (its scientific name is *Gryllidae*) is harmless. It also has no practical purpose—with one exception. By its chirps, the snowy tree cricket (*Oecanthus niveus*) can tell you how cold it is outside. Here's the formula:

Count the number of chirps per minute. Subtract 40. Divide this number by 4. Add 50, and you'll have the outdoor temperature in Fahrenheit.

It seems odd, but it works. Crickets are sensitive to changes in air temperature, so they chirp more slowly as the outdoor temperature drops, or faster as the outdoor temperature rises.

IT'S POSSIBLE TO AVOID A HANGOVER

HOW TRUE IS IT?
RAISE A GLASS TO THE OLD WIVES.

We humans have been very fond of a drink ever since we first discovered the skills of brewing about 4,000 years ago. This means that humans have also been trying to tackle their consequent hangovers for the last few millennia. This has given rise to much drink-related folklore, including what to drink to avoid the morning-after misery. Some cultures swear that the order of drinks is the essential factor; if you start with beer and move on to wine, no problem. But if you start with wine and progress to beer, expect disaster.

There is some truth to this in that different types of alcohol can give rise to more or less severe effects. Clear alcoholic drinks such as gin, vodka, and Japanese sake (rice wine) are less likely to cause a hangover. Some experts claim that the darker the alcohol, the more likely it is to punish you the next day. This is thought to be due to the presence of congeners, complex organic molecules. Darker drinks contain more congeners; hence brandy, red wine, and dark rum are all notorious for producing particularly bad hangovers.

Of course, the other major factor in this is the quantity that you drink. Downing a bottle of vodka in the course of one evening is unlikely to keep you clear-headed the next day, no matter how clear the alcohol.

Maybe the moral is that we should just accept that the unpleasantness of a hangover—the thumping headache, dry mouth, dizziness, and nausea—are the price we have to pay for overindulging. Edzard Ernst, a researcher from Peninsula

Medical School at the universities of Exeter and Plymouth in the UK, conducted a review of clinical trials into preventing or treating hangovers. He found that the majority of trials showed no beneficial effects. Ernst believes that a surefire hangover cure is unlikely ever to be found, and points out the ethical dilemma that would arise if one did come on the market: "It could lead to people drinking more alcohol because they think it is harmless."

Ernst adds: "A hangover is nature's way of saying alcohol is bad for you. The most effective way to avoid the symptoms of a hangover is to practice abstinence and moderation."

TORNADOES CANNOT CROSS A RIVER

HOW TRUE IS IT?
THAT'S SOME TWISTER-ED
LOGIC.

*A*wesome, erratic, and very, very dangerous, tornadoes have fascinated people even before the legendary twister struck Kansas in *The Wizard of Oz*. And, as tends to be the case with such a powerful force of nature, a lot of mythology has grown up around tornadoes.

According to the *Glossary of Meteorology*, a tornado is "a violently rotating column of air...often (but not always) visible as a funnel cloud" that has contact with both the ground and the clouds.

Local legends claim that certain places are safe because tornadoes peter out in a canyon, or cannot climb a hill or mountain, or cannot cross a river. According to Roger Edwards of the U.S. Storm Prediction Center, all these assertions are just plain wrong. At Salt Lake City, Utah, on August 11, 1999, a tornado went down one side of a canyon and up another without losing its destructive power. In 1989, a tornado thundered up the Grand Teton Mountains, leaving a swath of destruction 60 miles (130 kilometers) long. Without a moment's hesitation, tornadoes have blown across the Mississippi and the Ohio Rivers. In fact, the deadliest tornado ever to strike the United States, the notorious Tri-State Tornado of March 18, 1925, roared across the Mississippi River from Missouri to Illinois. Before it was over, the tornado had killed 695 people.

Another old wives' tale says that tornadoes do not strike cities. Tell that to the citizens of St. Louis, Missouri, Topeka, Kansas, Lubbock, Texas, and Denver, Colorado, all of which have seen tornadoes come roaring through their city streets. Finally, there is the modern myth that tornadoes are drawn to trailer parks. First of all, and most obviously, tornadoes do not have intelligence, or personality, or any other faculty that would enable them to choose where to strike. According to Hampton Sides, editor of *Outside* magazine's "The Wild File" column, the impression that tornadoes go after trailer parks is based on the tragically high death toll among trailer residents when their park is hit. Because trailers are not built on a foundation, they are more likely to be torn apart or thrown about by the force of a tornado. That explains why, in 1994, 40 percent of all Americans who died in a tornado lived in a trailer—this in spite of the fact that trailers account for only 6 percent of housing in the United States.

SUICIDES PEAK BETWEEN CHRISTMAS AND NEW YEAR

HOW TRUE IS IT?
YOU MIGHT AS WELL
BELIEVE THAT REINDEER
CAN FLY.

M any contemporary old wives maintain that the stress, anxiety, and loneliness of the holidays drive many unhappy individuals to suicide. But Dr. Herbert Hendin, medical director of the American Foundation for Suicide Prevention, says it just ain't so. He told a *New York Daily News* reporter, "I'd get calls every season from people who wanted to do a story on suicide and the holidays, and when I told them it wasn't true, they would get depressed!"

The National Center for Health Statistics confirms Dr. Hendin's claims. After studying the NCHS's cause-of-death data over a period of years, Dr. Hendin found that December is actually the lowest month of the year for suicides. January is pretty close to the bottom, too. Many psychiatrists believe the rate is so low at Christmas because it is a season when people tend to be more in touch with each other than at any other time of the year.

So what season does see the highest suicide rate? Surprisingly, spring and summer. Why would more people take their lives when the weather is beautiful and all of nature is burgeoning? The experts don't have an answer. Yet. But they have recognized the pattern, which explains why April is National Suicide Prevention Month.

Singapore's *The Straits Times* reports that in this nation-city that has no seasons, people tend to commit suicide on prominent holidays. Of the 300 to 400 suicides recorded in Singapore annually, most occur on the second day of Chinese New Year, New Year's Day, Christmas, Labor Day, or the Hindu holiday

Deepavali. Statistics in Singapore have found that holiday-related depression is not why people take their lives. Financial trouble is the leading cause for suicide among Singaporean men. About 33 percent kill themselves because they have lost money on an investment or through gambling, or have fallen deeply into debt.

According to *The Guardian* (London), Dr. Jan Birtle, a psychotherapist and lecturer in psychiatry at Birmingham University, has found that men are twice as likely to kill themselves as women. But attempted suicide is much more common among women—especially in the under-35s—than among men. Most often women blame relationship problems for their attempted suicide. Which brings us to a depressing statistic: in Birmingham, England, three casualty departments (known as emergency rooms in the United States) reported 69 women who had attempted suicide on Valentine's Day. This contrasts with fewer than 30 attempted suicides on two "neutral," or non-holiday, days selected from the calendar.

ANOTHER URBAN LEGEND

Dr. Harvey Roy Greenberg, a Manhattan psychiatrist and author of *Emotional Illness in the Family*, calls the Christmas suicide tale "a psychiatric urban myth." In this respect it is like other holiday myths—for example, the widespread phobia that at Halloween our neighbors start slipping razor blades into apples and sprinkling cyanide on candy. Alan Dundes, a professor of folklore at the University of California at Berkeley, says that the Halloween phobia is baseless, too, and urges people who don't believe him to check the police blotters.

BABY SNAKES ARE MORE POISONOUS THAN ADULTS

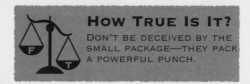

HOW TRUE IS IT?
DON'T BE DECEIVED BY THE SMALL PACKAGE—THEY PACK A POWERFUL PUNCH.

*H*umans are hard-wired to be terrified of snakes. But could the idea that baby snakes pack a more poisonous punch than their adults be just an extension of our fundamental reptile phobia? Actually, no. Baby snakes really are more deadly than adults. When a newborn venomous snake hatches, it is equipped with poison that is more potent than that of its parents.

Snake experts are not entirely certain why this is. One theory holds that because the baby snakes haven't bitten anything yet, their system has not had to regenerate more poison; thus, their venom is at full strength and much more dangerous. Another theory suggests that a high percentage of water is found in the venom of baby snakes that enables the poison to be absorbed more quickly into the victim's bloodstream.

On the bright side, a baby snake isn't as practiced as an adult at hurling itself at a victim—so it might miss you! And the baby snake's venom sac is smaller than a adult's, so the amount of venom injected into a victim is smaller.

Nonetheless, as Hampton Sides, editor of *Outside* magazine's "The Wild File" column, has found, a bite from a tiny baby diamondback rattlesnake can dissolve your tissue and leave a nasty permanent scar. And a baby copperhead has enough venom to burn right through your tissue down to the bone. If you are so unfortunate as to run across a nest of baby snakes, be afraid. And get out of there fast.

ARTHRITIS FLARES UP IN WET WEATHER

HOW TRUE IS IT?
THE ONLY THING THAT
FLARES UP IN WET
WEATHER IS YOUR PERM.

*A*rthritis sufferers will tell you that their pains flare up when the weather turns damp. But Donald A. Redelmeier, a professor of medicine at the University of Toronto, says it's unlikely that dampness would have any effect on arthritis. In the first place, Dr. Redelmeier says, the "skin surrounding joints is rather impervious to water and most people stay dry indoors during rain anyway. In addition, arthritis patients do not experience dramatic changes in their symptoms when immersed in water (such as during baths or swimming)."

Perhaps it's the drop in barometric pressure that causes the flare-ups. But Dr. Redelmeier finds that arthritis sufferers do not complain of increased pain during a plane flight or while driving a car through the mountains—two situations in which the body experiences greater swings in barometric pressure than when it rains.

Then maybe it's the humidity that's the culprit? Dr. Redelmeier doesn't buy that theory, either. "Hospitalized patients are often given humidified air to breathe," he says, "and this has little apparent effect on arthritis conditions." And he goes on to point out that taking a nice long shower will certainly fill the bathroom with humidity—yet arthritis patients don't regard showers as something to be avoided.

POLAR BEAR LIVER IS THE MOST POISONOUS THING TO EAT

HOW TRUE IS IT?
WELL, IT IS PRETTY
NASTY STUFF.

*T*here are worse things you could eat than polar bear liver. But in terms of making you deathly ill, if not outright dead, the old wives are absolutely right: this stuff will do the job.

Word of the dangers of eating polar bear liver got back to Europe in 1596. Willem Barentz, a Dutch explorer, and his men were exploring the Russian Arctic, searching for the Northeast Passage, the fabled water route to Asia. One day they shot and killed a polar bear for food. Several men who made the mistake of eating the liver died.

Polar bear liver is such a potent poison that just one bite will cause vomiting and dizziness. Eating a few pieces produces the hideous reaction of making the skin peel off, and then you die. The Inuits who live in the Arctic have known since time out of mind about the dangers of polar bear liver. When hunters kill a bear, they bury the liver deep so that their dogs won't find it. What made the bear's liver lethal remained a mystery until the 1940s. Then, two British biochemists studied polar bear liver and found it contained dangerous levels of vitamin A. Most of the animals polar bears hunt for food are rich in vitamin A.

The polar bear needs this vitamin for the same reason people do: to maintain healthy eyesight, skin, bones, and hair. But we don't have to worry as much about finding our next meal, whereas the polar bear must store large amounts of vitamin A in case it doesn't come across a vitamin-rich tasty morsel in the near future. So nature has given the polar bear a high tolerance for large amounts of vitamin A. Then the animal's liver filters vitamin A from its bloodstream and preserves it for future use. However, human livers were not designed for the rigors of arctic life, nor did nature intend for us to consume an entire seal in one sitting. Doing so would make us gluttons, not to mention sick.

The polar bear, however, cannot be sure where his next seal will be coming from and is built to feast when he can. By the way, the toxicity of polar bear liver is intensified if it is eaten with alcohol. So forget about washing down that polar bear pâté with a nice 1996 Rioja.

HANG UP A HORSESHOE FOR GOOD LUCK

HOW TRUE IS IT?
THE MYTH IS WIDESPREAD,
BUT NOT WELL-FOUNDED.

*O*ld wives in ancient Rome assured homeowners and shopkeepers that witches and evil spirits dreaded iron. A few iron nails tacked around a doorway were sure to keep a house or business free from malign influences. This idea merged with another old wives' tale, the belief that blacksmiths possessed magical powers. After all, they could take a lump of crude metal and turn it into a host of useful objects. Including, of course, iron horseshoes. That is how the horseshoe came to replace the iron nail as a good-luck emblem over the doorway of a house.

Examples of trust in the power of the horseshoe can be found all across Europe and North America. In Northumberland in England, the horseshoe not only drove off bad luck; the number of nail holes in the shoes told an unmarried man or woman who found it in how many years he or she would marry.

In the northernmost regions of Scotland, it was said that a horseshoe should be set up between the homes of two quarreling neighbors to neutralize the curses they hurled at each other. Seafarers from Scandinavia kept a horseshoe onboard ship to ward off lightning, the horseshoe being a survival from the old pagan Norse practice of sacrificing a horse before any major endeavor to win the favor of the gods.

The one major point upon which old wives disagree is how to hang the horseshoe. In Germany and the United States the shoe hangs upwards so that the luck doesn't run out. In other parts of Europe, however, the horseshoe is hung pointing downward so the good luck will flow into the house.

Farriers, horse owners, and horseshoe pitchers apparently do not put much stock in this old wives' tale. Given how much time these people spend around horseshoes, they would probably be in the best position to benefit from any good luck the horseshoe had to offer. In reality, horseshoes have caused more than a few mishaps, usually because of human error, not bad luck. Many horses have sustained serious injuries because they have been poorly shod. Many a farrier has been kicked by a dissatisfied horse.

Horseshoes have been around for a long time. They make horses' lives easier and can be fun to play with. But they won't bring you good luck, no matter which way round you hang them on your door.

CLUB SODA REMOVES RED WINE STAINS

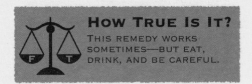

HOW TRUE IS IT?
THIS REMEDY WORKS
SOMETIMES—BUT EAT,
DRINK, AND BE CAREFUL.

*I*t's an article of faith among housekeepers that if someone spills red wine on the carpet or the tablecloth, you should dowse the area with club soda and the stain will come out. According to the folklore, it's the carbonation (the bubbles) in the club soda that makes the stain float miraculously away.

Writing in *Scientific American* magazine, Pete Wishnok, a chemist at the Massachusetts Institute of Technology, said that there was really nothing in club soda that would cause it to act as a stain remover. It's just water, carbon dioxide, and some salt. "It is weakly acidic," Professor Wishnok says, "so it might decolorize stains."

Drawing on his own experience, Professor Wishnok believes that the secret is not the club soda but the fabric upon which the red wine has been sloshed. He has successfully removed red wine from his carpet many times. "Our carpet is a synthetic that absorbs stains slowly," Professor Wishnok explained, "so—if you get there quickly with lots of paper towels—the club soda simply acts as a carrier to help blot everything up. Water would probably work as well, but club soda is more fun."

However, when red wine was spilled on his tablecloth, the club soda was much less effective. Professor Wishnok concludes that this is because the tablecloth was made of natural fibers and is not as thick as a carpet, so it absorbed the wine quickly.

COWS LIE DOWN BEFORE IT RAINS

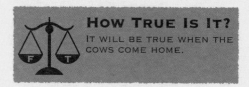

HOW TRUE IS IT?
IT WILL BE TRUE WHEN THE
COWS COME HOME.

*M*any of the old wives' tales center on the weather,
particularly weather forecasting. There are many legends
claiming that animals have a great sensitivity to imminent
changes in the weather, so knowing what changes in behavior to
look out for can tell you what weather conditions to expect.

One adage maintains that if cows are lying down in a field, it's
about to rain. The theory behind this seems to be that cows,
along with other animals, are sensitive to the fall in air pressure
that means rain or storms are on their way. So what does it
mean if half the cows are lying down and half of them are still
standing? The farmers have this one covered—"showers!"

Birds are also claimed to be reliable weather forecasters. Birds
fly high in the sky when there is fair weather, so the theory
goes, but falling air pressure causes discomfort in their ears, so
they fly low to alleviate it. Large numbers of birds roosting on
power lines is also thought to indicate falling air pressure. Other
renowned forecasters in the animal kingdom are bees, who
stay close to their hives when rain threatens, and spiders, who
abandon their webs before the rain comes.

And how accurate are they? It's certainly an attractive idea, but
it's hard to prove, especially as most of us live in cities when it's
easier to turn to the weather forecast in the newspaper than to
seek out cows and bees for a weather report.

CRACKING YOUR KNUCKLES CAUSES ARTHRITIS

HOW TRUE IS IT?
YOUR KNUCKLES ARE
PRETTY SAFE—BUT YOU
MIGHT SEND SHIVERS
DOWN SOMEONE'S SPINE.

*T*here's an urban legend among bone specialists about a kid who had been told that if he continued to crack his knuckles he'd get arthritis. In the interests of science, the kid became his own guinea pig. For years he cracked the knuckles of just one of his hands. When he was all grown up and had become a doctor, he X-rayed his hands to see if the knuckle-cracking one showed any susceptibility for arthritis. Not only did he see no sign of incipient arthritis, he found no discernible physical difference between his two hands.

This is folklore nirvana: perhaps the one and only occasion when an old wives' tale is debunked by an urban legend. Like the boy wonder of the urban legend, medical science has found no link between knuckle-cracking and arthritis. Furthermore, rare individuals who can bend their thumbs back until they touch their wrists are in no more danger than anyone else of arthritis. What these life-of-the-party people do have is ligamentous laxity, which just means that their ligaments enjoy greater flexibility than is the case with most of us. As orthopedic surgeon Dr. Donald Longjohn puts it, "Some people are a little more loose than others."

But even ligamentous laxity has its limits. Folks who can dislocate their shoulders or pop some other joint at will really are asking for trouble. Repeatedly popping a joint in and out of its socket does damage the joint. Once a joint becomes unstable, it is impossible to reverse the problem.

It's possible that the old wives' tale about cracking your knuckles is based on a hunch that repeating a certain action will damage your body. And it is true that there are repetitive tasks that can lead to arthritis. The act of driving large, hard-to-steer, heavy equipment such as a school bus puts everyday pressure on certain joints, and that can lead to arthritis.

But knuckle-crackers don't get off scot-free. Two researchers, Jorge Castellanos and David Axelrod, of Toledo, Ohio, published the results of their study of long-term knuckle-cracking in the *Annals of Rheumatic Diseases*. Castellanos and Axelrod found that people over age 45 who were still cracking their knuckles suffered from swollen hands and had lost some of the strength and sureness of their grip. Knuckle-cracking over a long period overstretches, and may even tear, the ligaments in the fingers. This can develop into swelling and loss of hand strength.

It's Bad Luck to Kill a Spider

How True Is It?

SORRY, MISS MUFFET, BUT THEY'RE NICER TO HAVE AROUND THAN YOU THINK.

*T*here are somewhere in the neighborhood of 35,000 species of spiders, and almost without exception they are nasty, aggressive, predatory, cannibalistic little beasts that will kill and eat anything that makes the mistake of wandering into their territory. That includes members of the spider's own immediate family. Clearly, then, we can only do good by squashing spiders wherever we find them, and the old wives' tale that encourages us to make nice with these eight-legged pests is way off the mark. Right?

Well, actually, no. Spiders that live in the corners of a house prey on many of the insects that make us humans miserable—most notably mosquitoes and cockroaches. Furthermore, science is discovering new uses for spider silk.

Most spiders spin a line of silk as they move about, just in case they have to make a sudden drop to escape a predator (just like Spiderman). The smaller species of spiders migrate by spinning a long strand of silk and then letting air currents carry it to a new habitat. Female spiders often create a silk sac in which to carry their eggs. Spiders that live underground close off the entrance to their burrow with a silk trapdoor. And some male spiders use their silk to tie up a female during the mating season. The spiders aren't getting kinky: female spiders are often larger than the males, and the lady spider in question may decide she would prefer the male courting her as a meal instead of a mate.

All of these varied uses for spider silk, not to mention its strength and resiliency, have intrigued scientists. At the University of Wyoming at Laramie a team of researchers led by Professor Randy Lewis has succeeded in discovering the formula by which spiders convert liquid proteins into silk. Dr. Lewis and his team are trying to create a synthetic spider silk that is stronger and more flexible than the one spiders produce.

One possibility for synthetic spider silk is body armor. The plastic known as Kevlar that is used today for body armor is extremely strong, "but it's not very stretchy," as Todd Blackledge, an entomologist at the University of Akron, puts it. The researchers are hoping to develop a body armor that feels and fits more like Lycra.

But synthetic spider silk could have many other uses as well, especially in medicine, where the extremely thin silk could be used to make extremely thin sutures for eye or nerve surgery.

Another unexpected possibility for synthetic spider silk is air bags. "Right now an air bag just blasts you back into a seat," said Dr. Lewis. "But if it were made out of this material it would actually be made to absorb energy and really reduce impact."

The researchers still have a long way to go. At this stage, synthetic spider silk doesn't replicate the strength of real spider silk, and the synthetic threads are too thick. But researchers such as Dr. Blackledge and Dr. Lewis are confident that they will get the formula right in time.

EATING CHOCOLATE MAKES YOU HAPPY

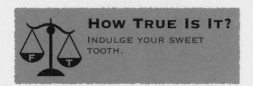

HOW TRUE IS IT?
INDULGE YOUR SWEET TOOTH.

We humans have long realized the beneficial effects that chocolate has on our mood. The botanical name for the cacao plant from which we derive chocolate is *Theobroma cacao*; "Theobroma" is Greek for "food of the gods." The ancient Mayans also elevated chocolate to a divine level: they had a god of cacao, Ek Chuah, to whom they would sacrifice a dog with chocolate-colored markings every April.

These days, myths about chocolate center around how it recreates the feeling of being in love. Chocolate stimulates endorphin production, which induces pleasurable feelings, and contains the stimulants caffeine and theobromine.

As well as boosting your mood, chocolate may also have medicinal benefits. Peter Barnes, professor of thoracic medicine at Imperial College London, UK, led a study that suggested that theobromine, may be a more effective cough medicine than traditional remedies. The researchers believe that theobromine acts on the sensory nerve endings of the vagus nerve, which runs through the airways in the lungs to the brain.

A study conducted at the University of Glasgow also indicates that eating chocolate (specifically dark chocolate) can boost the level of heart-protecting antioxidants in the blood. Antioxidants are involved in lowering the levels of free radicals in the blood. Exposure to free radicals has been linked to increased risk of cardiovascular disease and some cancers.

TUESDAYS ARE UNLUCKY

HOW TRUE IS IT?
IT HAS A CERTAIN HISTORY,
BUT IT IS STRICTLY
SUPERSTITION.

*T*hroughout most of the Western world Friday is considered unlucky, but among the Greeks Tuesday is dreaded as the unluckiest day of the week. They have a good reason for this superstition: on Tuesday, May 29, 1453, Constantinople fell to the Turks, and the last Byzantine emperor, Constantine XI, died fighting in defense of his city. The disaster marked the end of the Greek empire in the Eastern Mediterranean and the beginning of more than 400 years of near-slavery for the Greeks under the Turks.

The Greeks should have seen it coming. The Byzantine Empire, which once stretched through Asia Minor to Egypt and across North Africa, had shrunk to a sliver of what is now Turkey, and the mainland and islands of Greece. Recognizing that their capital was no longer a going concern, many inhabitants of Constantinople emigrated elsewhere, with the result that large portions of the city were virtually uninhabited. The city's triple ring of defensive walls still stood, but were in a bad state of disrepair. After enduring 54 days of assaults and relentless artillery bombardments by a Turkish army, Constantinople fell.

To this day, Greeks consider it unlucky to start any new business venture or project on a Tuesday. Many Greeks will not even enter a new shop on a Tuesday. Which makes the "Tuesday is unlucky" old wives' tale a self-fulfilling prophecy.

WALKING UNDER A LADDER IS BAD LUCK

HOW TRUE IS IT?
TRUE ENOUGH THAT YOU
SHOULD TAKE THOSE EXTRA
STEPS AND WALK AROUND.

The old wives' tale that it is bad luck to walk under a ladder is one of those stories that brings together superstition and common sense. The oldest roots of the superstition may go back to the early centuries of Christianity. A ladder leaning against a wall makes a triangle, and a triangle is a symbol of the Holy Trinity. To walk under a ladder, then, is to desecrate the symbol that represents the Father, the Son, and the Holy Spirit, and to align yourself with the devil.

But there is a problem with the logic of this superstition. The symbol of the Holy Trinity is an equilateral triangle in which all three sides are of equal length because all three Persons of the Trinity are equal. But a ladder leaning against a wall creates a right-angled triangle in which the three sides are of unequal length. In terms of the theology of the Trinity, this type of triangle is flagrantly heretical. So, one could interpret walking under a ladder as a symbolic poke in the eye of heresy.

Theological hair-splitting aside, the ladder superstition lives on. A 2003 study conducted in the United Kingdom found that refusal to walk under a ladder is the third most commonly held superstition, right behind knocking on wood (first place) and crossing one's fingers (second place).

Now, while it is true that a stroll under a ladder will not endanger your soul, the potential dangers to your body are alarming. The American Academy of Orthopedic Surgeons has found that 500,000 people in the United States are treated for ladder-related injuries every year. Furthermore, approximately

300 of these injuries proved to be fatal. The United Kingdom sees more than 40,000 ladder accidents annually, and about 50 ladder-related deaths.

Accidents range from those caused by ladders that have been placed on an unstable surface to ladders set against a wall at an unsafe angle; from climbers who are up too high and lose their balance or fall because their shoes are slick with grease or mud, to dropped buckets and tools that strike unwary passers-by.

The Bureau of Labor Statistics in Sweden found that 80 percent of all ladder accidents involved a fall; 73 percent involved do-it-yourselfers who did not know how to use a ladder safely; 57 percent involved individuals who had been trying to climb the ladder while holding a tool or some other object in one or both hands; and 30 percent involved climbers who simply slipped and fell. Clearly, the old wives were right: with all those ladders collapsing, climbers falling, and tools, buckets, and all manner of paraphernalia dropping to the ground, only a fool would walk under a ladder.

IF THE BABY IS LATE, TAKE LONG WALKS

HOW TRUE IS IT?
ANYONE WHO'D BUY THIS
ONE SHOULD TAKE A HIKE.

Old wives have tremendous sympathy for pregnant women, hence the large number of pregnancy-related myths. The leaders of this particular pack are two genres of old wives' tales: "How to Tell the Baby's Gender" and "How to Get the Baby to Come Out."

There are women who blithely declare that they had easy pregnancies, and that they felt fine during the whole nine months. One prays these insensitive ladies do not make such comments in front of women who suffered months of back, leg, and groin pain from lugging all that extra weight around, are now past their due date, and just want the damn kid to be born already. As you'd expect, the old wives offer remedies that will encourage the unborn child to get the ball rolling.

Expectant mothers are told that taking long walks can help induce labor. Dr. Jonathan Schaffir, a clinical assistant professor of obstetrics and gynecology at the Ohio State University Medical Center, found that two out of three pregnant women believed walking brings on labor. In December 2000 he interviewed 102 pregnant women from the region around Columbus, Ohio, asking their opinions of ten common recommendations on how to get the baby to come. Of those 102 expectant moms, 84 percent had heard that walking worked, and 64 percent believed it was true.

Those women were indulging in a little wishful thinking. Walking does not induce labor. In fact, the staff of the Mayo Clinic has stated bluntly, "No one knows for sure what triggers labor—and every woman's experience is unique." All that can be said for certain is that there are typical symptoms that tell a woman her body is getting ready to go into labor. These signs include the baby settling deeper into the mother's pelvis, the softening, thinning, or dilation of the cervix, and even a sudden burst of energetic housekeeping known as "nesting."

Another common old wives' tale is that having sex will bring the baby. This one is regarded with such certainty that it has a corollary old wives' tale: if the mother has sex early in her pregnancy, she runs the risk of miscarriage or premature delivery. A study published by the American College of Obstetrics and Gynecology found that having sex does *not* increase miscarriages, premature deliveries, or hasten the delivery of the full-term child.

Some old wives encourage mothers to eat spicy food to jump-start childbirth. More often than not, the following day the mother has heartburn, not a new baby.

Castor oil is another popular folk remedy to move nature along. And here the old wives may have been on to something. Castor oil can cause contractions, but researchers have found that it can cause such severe contractions as to harm the unborn child.

What does Dr. Schaffir recommend? "For healthy pregnancies, Mother Nature is the best obstetrician," he advises. "These things take time."

IF THE HANGMAN'S ROPE BREAKS, THE PRISONER IS INNOCENT

HOW TRUE IS IT?
NOT VERY.

*I*n earlier times, the public execution of a criminal followed a set pattern. The spectators lined the way to the gallows to see how the condemned carried himself (or herself), then crowded around the scaffold to hear their last words. After the execution of a particularly notorious lawbreaker, it was common for printers to capitalize on the occasion by churning out cheap pamphlets, complete with illustrations, that described the felon's last moments.

The spectators at a public hanging might differ in opinion as to the guilt of the condemned, but there was one point on which they all agreed: if the hangman's rope snapped, it was a sign from God that the prisoner was innocent and he had to be set free. Apparently no one argued that the rope was weak, or the condemned too heavy, or that the hangman somehow hadn't done his job properly. Divine intervention was the only explanation for a broken rope.

The roots of this old wives' tale go back at least 4,000 years to a legal concept known as trial by ordeal. The idea is simple: God will not permit an innocent person to be punished and will intervene with a miracle to protect the innocent from harm. The Romans, however, rejected as ridiculous the idea that a trial by ordeal would prove anything. But the barbarian tribes, especially in Germany, were big advocates of ordeals. Ordeals took several forms. One was a duel, with the accused and the accuser fighting it out until one was dead.

Another option called for red-hot irons. In this case, the accused walked nine feet holding a red-hot iron in his hand, or walked barefoot over nine red-hot plowshares. If his skin was not burned, he was considered innocent.

A third popular option was the water ordeal. The accused was tied hand and foot and thrown into a pond or some other body of water. If he sank, he was considered guilty.

Even after the Germans converted to Christianity, the ordeal endured, in spite of frequent condemnations by the popes who objected strongly to the notion that one could strong-arm God into acting as a referee in humankind's petty disputes.

During the reign of Henry II, England stopped relying on ordeals except in cases where no other means for proving guilt or innocence were available—murders without witnesses, or the alleged use of witchcraft, for example. In 1215, the Fourth Lateran Council ordered Catholic priests to stop using trials by ordeal. Adhering to this council's ruling, Henry III brought ordeals to a halt in England in 1220, replacing them with jury trials. By the Age of Enlightenment, the practice of ordeals had ended in Western Europe.

Anecdotal evidence, however, indicates that trial by ordeal was not merely arbitrary. Notions of justice predate the modern era and many people survived trials by ordeal, often because a priest, probably noting that the evidence supported the innocence of the defendant or based on an assessment of the accused's character, intervened and determined the outcome of an ordeal. Ordeals, unlike our present legal system, appeared to begin with the assumption that a person was guilty until proven innocent, not vice versa.

GINGER ALE SOOTHES
A QUEASY STOMACH

HOW TRUE IS IT?
THIS ONE'S BASED ON
FIZZY LOGIC.

*I*n January 1988, the late President Ronald Reagan was looking forward to a luncheon visit with Japanese Prime Minister Noboru Takeshita when he was struck down by a stomach virus. By the time the Japanese Prime Minister arrived at the White House, Reagan was feeling well enough to greet his guest and join him for lunch. But while Takeshita dined on salmon bisque and breast of Cornish game hen, Reagan limited himself to consommé and flat ginger ale.

Ginger is thought to soothe a queasy stomach, but Dr. Don McConnell, an emergency pediatrician at Edmonton's University Hospital, has found that "most ginger ale has so little ginger it's not effective and the sugar in the pop makes diarrhea worse." Dr. Dianne Brox of the Alberta Medical Association agrees and suggests electrolyte drinks for kids and sport drinks or unsweetened herbal tea for nauseated teens and adults.

With stomach viruses, the dehydration brought on by bouts of vomiting or diarrhea is the greatest worry. Young children and the elderly are especially susceptible to dehydration and, as noted above, the sugar in ginger ale or other soft drinks only contributes to the problem. To restore the salts and minerals the ailing body needs at this time, sports drinks that replace electrolytes are the best option.

NUMBER THIRTEEN IS LUCKY OR UNLUCKY

HOW TRUE IS IT?
IT HAS A REPUTATION BOTH
WAYS, BUT NO SCIENCE ON
ITS SIDE.

*I*n virtually every part of the Christian world, old wives recoil at the number 13. It is not uncommon to find airliners that don't have a 13th row, or hotels that don't have a 13th floor. We'll explore the origins of this accursed number when we examine Friday the 13th, but for the moment, let's look at one group that regards 13 as lucky: the Greeks.

The way the Greeks see it, 13 represents Christ plus his twelve apostles. Seen in that light, how could such a number be bad? True, Greeks who have emigrated from their homeland, and their descendants, generally have adopted the more common phobia about number 13. But back in the Old Country, Greeks continue to regard 13 as a number top-heavy with good omens. And recently their faith in the inherent goodness of 13 was rewarded: at the Sydney Olympics in 2000, Greece had its best show ever, coming home with 13 medals.

WATER GOES DOWN CLOCKWISE IN THE SOUTHERN HEMISPHERE

HOW TRUE IS IT?
THIS ONE'S FALSE THE
WORLD OVER.

*I*t's said that in the Northern Hemisphere, water goes down the drain in a counterclockwise direction. In the Southern Hemisphere water goes down the drain in a clockwise direction. The reason, according to the old wives, is that the earth's rotation affects the direction in which water drains depending on which side of the Equator you're on.

But it is simply not true. Fred W. Decker, Professor Emeritus of Oceanic and Atmospheric Science at Oregon State University, says, "Really, I doubt that the direction of the draining water represents anything more than an accidental twist given by the starting flow."

Robert Ehrlich, a physicist at George Mason University, says that even if there is anecdotal evidence of bathtubs draining in different directions, it isn't the pull of the earth's rotation that is the cause. "In your tub," says Dr. Ehrlich, "such factors as any small asymmetry of the shape of the drain will determine in which direction the circulation occurs. Even in a tub having a perfectly symmetric drain, the circulation direction will be primarily influenced by any residual currents in the bathtub left over from the time when it was filled."

Some old wives may object, arguing that the direction water swirls down a drain is determined by the Coriolis effect. But they're indulging in pseudoscience. The Coriolis effect is an apparent force that, due to the Earth's rotation, deflects moving bodies that have an established direction of motion—like air and ocean currents and projectiles—to the right in the Northern

Hemisphere and to the left in the Southern Hemisphere. Water in a bathtub doesn't have an established direction until you pull the plug, so the Coriolis effect simply doesn't come into play..

But the old wives don't give up so easily. They have pointed out that cyclones in the Northern Hemisphere swirl about in a counterclockwise direction, whereas cyclones in the Southern Hemisphere rotate in a clockwise direction. Once again we turn to Dr. Ehrlich for an answer. He says that the direction a cyclone takes is the result of "interactions between moving masses of air and air masses moving with the rotating earth." Remember that a cyclone is an immense storm system that covers a large piece of territory. It stands to reason that the effects, or the pull, of the earth's rotation will be "much more pronounced when the circulation covers a larger area than would occur inside your bathtub."

To See a Magpie Means You're About to Marry

How True Is It?
DON'T BOOK THE CATERER
JUST YET.

*T*he magpie is regarded as a bird of marriage, happiness, and good luck in China. Magpies sing beautifully. Hearing a flock of them singing together is one of life's little pleasures. No wonder that in traditional Chinese culture, to hear a magpie sing is a sign that happiness is on its way.

The Manchu Chinese regard the magpie as sacred. Legend tells how the goddess Fokulon once saw a beautiful magpie with a red fruit in its mouth flying above her. As the bird flew overhead it dropped the fruit. Fokulon picked it up, ate it, and soon found she was pregnant. She gave birth to a boy whom she named Bukulirongshun: he became the ancestor of the Manchus.

The magpie's connection with marriage comes from another Chinese legend. The emperor's youngest daughter fell in love with a cowherd. When the emperor learned of the affair, he exiled the lovers to opposite ends of the sky, and ordered a vast band of stars to keep the cowherd and the princess apart. But a flock of magpies took pity on the lovers and built an enchanted bridge so the couple could be together forever.

It's a lovely story, but in real life magpies are not an especially good model for marriage. Magpies are social birds, generally living in groups that range in number from three to 24. This group is not a happy, extended family; it is a harem. Only one of the birds in the group is male, and he mates with all the females

AN APPLE A DAY KEEPS THE DOCTOR AWAY

HOW TRUE IS IT?
YOUR HMO WILL BE THRILLED: APPLES HAVE TREMENDOUS HEALTH BENEFITS.

*P*lenty of medical evidence from around the world backs up what old wives have been saying for generations: you can derive a host of health benefits from apples.

Researchers at the agricultural school of Hirosaki University found that juice made from small, immature apples are packed with antioxidants known as polyphenols—up to 10 times the amount of polyphenols found in fully ripe apples. These polyphenols encourage the production of natural-killer (NK) cells which target cancer cells.

But apples can do much more. For example, the juice in apples interacts with gastric juices in the stomach to reduce intestinal disorders. The sugar in apples does not raise a body's blood sugar level, which means the fruit is effective in preventing diabetes. Apples can also prevent heart disease by reducing the level of bad cholesterol and boosting the body's good cholesterol.

Dr. Chang Y. Cy Lee, a professor of food science at Cornell University in New York, reports that apples contain quercetin, a chemical compound that can protect brain cells from the damage caused by such diseases as Alzheimer's and Parkinson's. Meanwhile, researchers at London's Kings College and University of Southampton in England are studying evidence that suggests quercetin can reduce the risk of contracting lung diseases such as asthma, bronchitis and emphysema.

WE'RE SIX DEGREES AWAY FROM EVERYONE ELSE

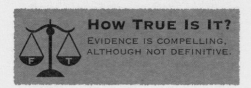

HOW TRUE IS IT?
EVIDENCE IS COMPELLING,
ALTHOUGH NOT DEFINITIVE.

*I*t was the John Guare play and movie, *Six Degrees of Separation*, that popularized the otherwise obscure idea that all humankind is mysteriously linked together. The father of this old wives' tale was a Hungarian writer, Frigyes Karinthy. Back in 1929 he conjectured that there are only five intermediary individuals between you and everyone else on Earth.

Karinthy's notion became known as the "Small World Problem," and his theory of linkages as "six degrees of separation." The idea is appealing, but it wasn't until the 1950s that anyone tried to prove it. Manfred Kochen, a mathematician, and Ithiel de Sola Pool, a political scientist, tried to find a mathematical solution. They suggested that if you were to choose 1,000 friends at random from 100 million people, then any two individuals would be separated by only two or three degrees of separation.

The Kochen-de Sola Pool method didn't hold water, however, because people do not choose their friends at random. In the 1960s, social psychologist Stanley Milgram and his graduate student Jeffrey Travers decided to test Karinthy's theory in a fresh way. They gave a letter to 300 individuals who lived either in Boston or Omaha. The letter was addressed to a stockbroker in Sharon, Massachusetts. Each person who received the letter was supposed to pass it on to someone he or she believed was closer to the target (as Milgram and Travers called the stockbroker). Of the 300 copies of the letter, 64 arrived in the stockbroker's mailbox. And on average, it took a chain of six people to get the letter to him. Hence the name for the theory, the phenomenon, the play, and the movie.

SIX DEGREES OF KEVIN BACON

Inspired by the John Guare play and movie, not to mention a little alcohol, in 1994 three Pennsylvania college students created a now-famous game: Six Degrees of Kevin Bacon. The students then appeared on a popular comedy television show. The rest, as they say, is history—and a website, book, and board game.

The students, Craig Fass, Brian Turtle, and Mike Ginelli, decided to use the actor Kevin Bacon to demonstrate that the world of actors is indeed small. Why Kevin Bacon, you ask? Well, the three young men must have learned something about scanning poetry from their English professors. His name contains the same number of syllables as the word "separation" and employs a similar rhythm. Bacon, they also reasoned, by virtue of having appeared in numerous ensemble films, could be linked to all other actors by no more than six degrees.

Try it, using any actor you want. Start with this person and count the steps it takes you to get to Kevin Bacon. Once you get to six, however, you have to stop. Six Degrees of Kevin Bacon neither proves nor disproves theories about linkages. But it is a fun way to test your knowledge of movie trivia.

Writing in *Scientific American* magazine, Duncan J. Watts, an associate professor of sociology at Columbia University, says Milgram and Travers' experiment is intriguing. But the matter has yet to be settled, and probably never will be: a definitive study would require surveying the whole of humanity.

BREAKING A MIRROR BRINGS SEVEN YEARS' BAD LUCK

HOW TRUE IS IT?
IT'S NOTHING TO WORRY
ABOUT BEYOND THE
SHARDS.

Nothing fills the old wives with horror quite like the sight of a shattered mirror. Two superstitions come together in this old wives' tale: the notion that the mirror catches the reflection of the soul, and the ancient Roman belief that every person is essentially remade, body and soul, every seven years. And some New Age philosophers subscribe to a similar belief, contending that our cells regenerate every seven years.

Almost from the moment mirrors were invented (more than 4,000 years ago), people from Egypt to China to Mexico believed that the image they saw in the glass was not just a reflection of the human form, but also a glimpse of the individual's soul. This belief led to a host of precautionary measures. Mirrors were covered at night or during an illness because, some traditions held, the soul of a sleeping or sick person left the body and traipsed about the world. A restless soul, free from its body, would not see its reflection and become trapped for all eternity in the glass. At the moment of death, mirrors were covered or turned toward the wall so that the soul would not make the mistake of moving toward the mirror instead of heading for eternal life in the next world. Years ago in Bulgaria this tradition was followed with almost religious zeal because Bulgarians believed if the soul of the newly departed became trapped in a mirror, it would wait there to steal the soul of the next living person who looked into the glass.

This connection of the mirror and the soul led to one of the best-known bits of vampire folklore. A vampire has no reflection in a mirror because, as one of the undead, a vampire has no soul.

The ancient Greeks were nervous around reflective pools of water. They believed that in such places lived malignant spirits eager to steal the soul of whoever looked at their reflection on the surface of the water. With the soul gone, the body, of course, would die. A version of this Greek myth survived in the legend of mermaids who seized unwary sailors, dragging them to their deaths at the bottom of the sea.

Probably it was the ancient Romans who associated seven years of bad luck with a broken mirror. Since the mirror reflected the soul, a shattered mirror would cause serious damage to the soul of the individual who broke it. The Romans believed that the body and soul changed every seven years, and so concluded that seven years would pass before the harm done by the broken mirror would be repaired. To save time, however, the Romans said that if you ground the broken mirror to dust so small that no reflection could be seen, then the whole seven years of bad luck would be nullified. African-American slaves found an easier way to get rid of the bad luck: they picked up all the broken pieces of the mirror, set them in a stream running south, and left them there for seven hours—long enough for all the bad luck to be washed away.

BURGLARS TARGET HOUSES AFTER A DEATH IN THE FAMILY

HOW TRUE IS IT?
IT'S BEEN KNOWN
TO HAPPEN.

ometimes the old wives get it right. There really are professional thieves who target the homes of the recently deceased, cleaning out the place on the very day of the departed's funeral.

A notorious case occurred in 1996 in Pasadena, California, where two seemingly nice, polite sisters robbed the homes of at least 40 dead people. The burglars, Helen Eposto, a 34-year-old nurse, and Jean Kolentik, a 32-year-old bookkeeper, had a system. In a black notebook they listed the names and addresses of who had died, who was away on vacation, or who was off on a honeymoon. In other words, they were getting their tips from the obituary page and the society column.

Although the police in Pasadena implicated the sisters in 40 residential burglaries, based on the enormous array of valuables they recovered, the cops were inclined to believe these women had robbed many more homes. "The loot," as Detective Ray Bartlett described it, filled an entire police storeroom. "And," he went on to say, "we've received calls from more than 300 persons who think they may have been victims of the sisters." Some of the stuff found in the sisters' house astonished the cops. They couldn't imagine how two small women could have hauled away massive color televisions and heavy floor safes.

Pasadena is not the only city plagued by opportunistic burglars. In November 2003, police in Akron, Ohio, attributed at least three break-ins to obituary-reading thieves. The problem is sufficiently widespread in the state of Washington to lead its attorney-general's office to include the following caveat on its website in a bold-faced font:

"BEWARE: Some burglars will burglarize the homes of deceased persons at the time of the funeral service. Make arrangements to guard the home during the funeral."

The sheriff's office in one Tennessee community offers to check its residents' homes during funerals—without charge. Numerous funeral homes provide instructions for bereaved families about practical matters such as death certificates; social security, veteran, and life insurance benefits; thank-you notes; cemetery markers—and thieves. And one security firm lists having a housesitter during funerals as a way to crimeproof a house. The two sisters in Pasadena, though remarkably good at their jobs, are hardly alone. Thieves will turn your misfortune into good luck for themselves, so get a house sitter, call a neighbor, or notify your local police before you leave for your loved one's funeral.

IT'S BAD LUCK TO KILL A LADYBUG

HOW TRUE IS IT?
THAT'S NO WAY TO TREAT
A LADY(BUG).

*I*f you lived in Europe during the Middle Ages you'd have been a fool to kill a ladybug. According to folklore, the ladybug was a favorite of the Virgin Mary. Through the ladybug, Mary was said to shower graces on good people: fine clothes, jewels, gold, and healthy babies. That last is why in some parts of Italy the ladybug was called *commaruccia*, which means "the little midwife." Consequently, anyone who killed a ladybug could expect be on the bad side of the Virgin Mary for nine days.

While a ladybug is not likely to bring you gold, jewels, or offspring, it is a very useful little creature nonetheless. Gardeners especially should be kind to ladybugs; they eat aphids, which damage roses; mites, which destroy new buds on flowers; mealy bugs, which thrive in greenhouses; and white flies, which attack house plants such as fuchsia. In vegetable gardens ladybugs target tomato worms, cabbage moths, and broccoli worms.

If you have insect trouble, you can buy packages of live ladybugs from mail order companies. It's easy to release them in an enclosed space such as a greenhouse, but releasing a cloud of ladybugs out in the garden is another matter. To encourage them to remain in the neighborhood, spray the package of ladybugs with a solution of water and any sugary soft drink, then spread them around your garden. The sticky solution will prevent them from flying away for a couple days—long enough for the ladybugs to realize there is plenty of food right where they are.

WOMEN CAN PROPOSE ON FEBRUARY 29

HOW TRUE IS IT?
LIKE LEAP YEAR, IT
HAPPENS OCCASIONALLY.

A common thread in folklore around the world asserts that taking decisive action on an extraordinary day can have positive consequences. Since February 29 comes around only once every four years, many societies believed that it was an auspicious day for conceiving or birthing babies, proposing marriage, or getting married.

In Europe, especially in the British Isles, February 29 is the day when women no longer have to wait for men to get up the nerve to propose marriage: ladies can pop the question themselves, without the risk of appearing ill-bred, or desperate. There are even bogus credentials for this custom. It's said that in 1228 Queen Margaret of Scotland decreed that any man who turned a woman down on February 29 would be fined £1. Another tradition, also from Scotland, says the Scots Parliament passed a law that if a man wouldn't marry the bold lassie who proposed to him, he had to make amends by giving her a silk gown or £100. And a third tradition says the right of women to pop the question is enshrined in English common law. They sound delightfully Old World, but don't be fooled: all of these laws are mythical. It's all very colorful, but it's also all nonsense.

In the ancient world, it was common for Celtic women to pop the question (and they did not wait until leap year). Today, of course, it is perfectly acceptable for a woman to ask her boyfriend to marry.

LISTENING TO LOUD MUSIC
CAUSES DEAFNESS

HOW TRUE IS IT?
THIS ONE HAS A
RESOUNDING RING
OF TRUTH.

One of the casualties of rock'n'roll is Pete Townsend: all those years spent playing guitar for The Who in front of massive blaring speakers damaged his auditory nerve. Townsend suffers from tinnitus, hearing loss that is often accompanied by a ringing or buzzing sound in the ears. The damage is permanent: there is no cure for tinnitus.

The sad story of Townsend, combined with a host of anecdotal evidence of club kids who report ringing in the ears even two days after they've been to a club or a rave, reinforces what old wives have been telling us for years: turn down the music or you'll go deaf.

All sound travels through the air as vibrations. These vibrations travel down the ear canal, through the eardrum, into the middle ear and finally into the cochlea, in the inner ear, where the vibrations are registered as sounds. Lining the inner ear are tiny, sensitive hairs. When they encounter vibrations, they shimmy like a 14-year-old girl at a Justin Timberlake concert.

Mind-numbingly loud noises at a high frequency can damage or even kill these tiny hairs and lead to hearing loss. What is especially scary is that no pain accompanies hearing loss, so there is no warning signal from the your body that you're in trouble.

A University of Florida study found that hearing loss is on the rise among young people. According to the university's researchers, 17 percent of 10-to-24-year-olds have already lost part of their hearing. The human ear can put up with long periods of noise in the 80-to-90 decibel range without being damaged. Yet people who work on road construction, where the noise level is in the generally acceptable 80-to-90 decibel range, wisely protect their ears with ear plugs. Anything above that, however, and all bets are off. The squeal of a subway, for example, measures at 96 decibels. That's not a cause for worry for most mass transit riders, says Janet Mackay, an audiologist at Montreal's Royal Victoria Hospital. But if while riding the subway the commuter is listening to a Walkman—which can play music at 110 decibels—then the risk of hearing trouble increases. Just imagine what happens at a club where the decibel level usually exceeds 120.

So listen to your mother: turn down that noise!

HOW LONG YOU CAN HEAR NOISES BEFORE IT STARTS TO BECOME A PROBLEM

The Sight & Hearing Association of the United States Occupational Safety and Health Administration has worked up this list of noises, their decibel levels, and how long you can put up with them without ear protection.

- Traffic noise, lawn mower   90 decibels   8 hrs.
- Motorcycle, power saw   95 decibels   4 hrs.
- Chain saw, train horn   100 decibels   2 hrs.
- Helicopter, jackhammer   105 decibels   1 hr.
- Snowmobile from the back   110 decibels   30 mins.
- Jet skis, crying baby   115 decibels   15 mins.
- Rock concert, sand blasting   120 decibels   less than 15 mins.

You'll Catch Cold If You Go Out With Wet Hair

HOW TRUE IS IT?
YOU MIGHT CATCH SOME
STRANGE LOOKS FROM
YOUR NEIGHBORS, BUT
NOT A COLD.

*T*he idea that walking around in winter weather with wet feet or wet hair will bring on a cold is one of the most firmly entrenched old wives' tales. For more than 100 years, scientists have been methodically debunking this myth, but this is one fable people just won't give up.

One of the world's top experts on the common cold, Dr. Jack M. Gwaltney, Jr., an emeritus professor of medicine at the University of Virginia, explains that, "Health and the weather was a big topic in previous periods of history." Scientists have noticed that some infectious diseases follow a seasonal pattern, but they don't understand why.

What scientists do know, however, is that a cold is caused by one of several hundred different strains of viruses that plague the planet. According to the United States National Institutes of Health, every year approximately one billion people worldwide suffer from colds. All these cold sufferers picked up the colds by coming into contact with a cold virus, either by touching something contaminated with cold-virus germs, such as a telephone or a stair rail, or by being near someone who had a cold and whose sneezing or coughing sprayed cold germs into the air. And that may account for winter being designated "cold and flu season": with more people confined together indoors, it is easier for the cold virus to spread.

After World War II researchers at the Common Cold Research Unit in Salisbury, England, recruited a dozen volunteers to take a bath, then wander up and down a cold corridor in wet socks and their bathing suits for as long as they could stand it. Their body temperature dropped a few degrees, and they felt pretty miserable, but in the end these damp dozen did not catch more colds than other people in the same building who had remained warm and dry.

In the 1950s in Chicago, researchers brought in 253 volunteers to see if being cold would indeed produce more colds. One group sat in a 60-degree Fahrenheit room in nothing but their socks and underwear. Another group sat in a freezer, bundled up in warm clothing. Both groups caught colds at exactly the same rate. Time and again researchers have returned to this question, and each time they have come to the same conclusion: being cold and wet doesn't increase your likelihood of catching a cold, nor will it make the cold you already have worse.

The data is remarkably consistent. If only the researchers could get people to believe it…

BEES AND WASPS
SENSE FEAR

HOW TRUE IS IT?
TRUE—IN A MANNER
OF SPEAKING.

When suddenly confronted by a swarm of bees or wasps, the old wives advise acting brave and standing absolutely still. Why? Because when bees and wasps sense fear, they attack.

Nature has not outfitted bees and wasps with fear-tracking radar, but it has given them the sense to recognize potentially threatening behavior. Remember that bees are programmed to protect the queen and the hive from intruders. If you inadvertently come near a hive, and then start hopping and flailing about in the usual manner of a human in the presence of bees, the bees are bound to interpret your actions as provocative. To make you go away, they will sting you.

Two other physical reactions are common among bee-phobic humans: we hyperventilate, and we break out in a sweat. According to U.S. Department of Agriculture entomologist Justin Schmidt, "If you're frightened, you exhale more carbon dioxide, and the odors of your sweat become more pungent." Bees pick this up and become agitated because, as Schmidt goes on to say, "Bees are one thousand times more sensitive to certain chemicals than we are."

So bees can certainly identify the telltale signs that we are scared of them. To get away from garden-variety bees and wasps, move very slowly. Chances are decent that you'll escape unstung. Contrary to popular belief, you don't have to travel to southern Africa to meet a swarm of killer bees, or Africanized Honeybees to use their formal name. They now live in southern Texas, New Mexico, and California as well as in Mexico, Central and South America. Unfortunately, killer bees look very much like other honeybees, so if you encounter a bee in one of these places, don't wait to find out where its ancestors hail from. Assume the worst, then move away and hold your breath—remember that carbon dioxide sets bees off. If a killer bee does sting you, however, then by all means panic and run very, very fast. Along with the pain of a killer bee's sting comes a pheromone that identifies you as a target for the rest of the hive.

Killer-bee stings are potentially life-threatening because you're likely to suffer multiple stings if you get too close to a colony of these aggressive, territorial, honey-producing insects. They don't want you around. They will chase you away and sting you if they can. So be cautious—but don't let the killer bees know you're afraid!

Dogs Can Smell Blood on a Murderer Years Later

HOW TRUE IS IT?
THE SCENT OF BLOOD
DOES INDEED LINGER,
BUT NOT FOR YEARS.

*T*he image of baying bloodhounds chasing a runaway is burned into our collective memory. As early as the 14th century, bloodhounds were being used to find fugitives. A bloodhound's sense of smell is 1,000 times more powerful than a human's. We have about five million smelling cells in our nasal passages; dogs about 220 million. Bloodhounds are blessed not only with millions of olfactory cells, but also with especially long noses, wide nostrils, and heads designed for serious smelling. This power lies at the root of the old wives' tale that dogs can smell human blood on the hands of a killer, even years after the crime.

As often happens in old wives' tales, a scrap of truth is being blown way out of proportion. Bloodhounds can follow a cold trail, perhaps as long as five days after the person being hunted has passed that way (assuming there hasn't been rain or snow or some other event that would make detecting the trail impossible). Within a few days of a violent crime, a bloodhound can detect traces of blood no human can see on a rug or splattered on a wall. But expecting a bloodhound to pick up the scent of blood years after a murder is asking a lot of the pooch.

Today all types of dogs are trained by police, military, and search-and-rescue organizations to trace the scent of survivors buried in the rubble of a building, people lost in an avalanche, or drugs or bombs hidden in a traveler's luggage.

GINGER AND SPRING ONION SOUP IS A GREAT FLU REMEDY

HOW TRUE IS IT?
STICK WITH THE
CHICKEN SOUP.

*F*eed a cold, starve a fever, is what old wives say in the West. But in China, starve a cold, starve a fever is the rule. Traditional Chinese healers argue that rich, nutritious foods will only strengthen the cold or flu and make it linger longer. Consequently, giving sick people a bowl of chicken soup is out of the question.

A classic Chinese cold and flu remedy is a soup made with ginger and the white part of a spring onion. The most important ingredient is the ginger, which is said to eliminate chills, reduce coughs and congestion, and soothe headaches and aching muscles. According to traditional Chinese medicine, ginger's hot, spicy quality generates sweat, thus pushing the virus out through the patient's pores. To meet the demand, both in the sickroom and in the kitchen, 2 million pounds of ginger are produced in Asia annually. But alas, there is no scientific data to support the supposed benefits of ginger for fighting a cold.

Ginger is good, however, for an upset stomach. Two tablespoons of thinly sliced fresh ginger root steeped for several minutes in a mug of boiling water will soothe the nausea that often accompanies flu or a bad cold. It also works well for stomach cramps, the queasiness associated with motion sickness and pregnancy, and indigestion.

THROW SPILLED SALT OVER YOUR SHOULDER FOR LUCK

HOW TRUE IS IT?
THIS IS ONE SALTY STORY.

*T*he old wives are very keen to protect us all from the ill winds of bad fortune. Many old wives' tales are concerned with staving off bad luck, and one of them says that if you spill salt at the dinner table, you should pick up a pinch and throw it over your left shoulder. They are particularly vehement that you throw it over your left side.

This tradition seems to stem from biblical times. Salt was a valuable commodity, traded ounce for ounce for gold. It was essential for preserving food, especially meat, at a time when there was no reliable method of refrigeration. Salt was so precious that Roman centurions were paid their wages partly in the condiment; the word "salary" derives from this tradition.

Because salt was so highly prized, spilling it was considered to be almost sacrilegious. Throwing some over your shoulder was thought to keep the devil at bay. The left side had a traditional association with evil or sinister things. This connection persists into modern times; the Latin word for left is *sinistra*, from where we derive the word "sinister."

Spilling salt may also have a connection with the morality tale of Lott's wife, who was turned into a pillar of salt when she looked back on Sodom. The tale reminds you to put the devil behind you or suffer the consequences. So does throwing salt bring you good luck? Probably not, but not spilling it in the first place would at least save you some housework.

YOU CAN CURE HICCUPS BY HOLDING YOUR BREATH

HOW TRUE IS IT?
DON'T GASP—THIS ONE
MIGHT JUST WORK.

*T*he old wives have a host of remedies for the quirky ailments that nature can inflict on us without warning, including hiccups.

Hiccups are typically caused by an involuntary spasm of the diaphragm—the thin muscle separating the lungs from the abdomen. It's not clear why they occur, but low levels of carbon dioxide in the bloodstream make hiccups worse, which suggests that their function may be to control respiration.

The logic behind the folklore cures for hiccups mostly involve trying to control your breathing so you interrupt the cycle of spasms. Some people swear by holding their breath and counting to seven. Holding the breath may help to stop hiccups by raising the concentration of carbon dioxide in the arteries.

Another old wives' remedy is to have someone drop a cold key down your back. The shock of the cold metal on your bare skin will cause you to gasp (so the old wives swear), and the sudden intake of breath may stop the cycle.

Some breast-feeding mothers have found that they can get their babies to stop hiccupping by suckling them. This suckling mechanism may explain why drinking a glass of water from the other side can help stop hiccups (you can only do it without spilling if you suck up the water). And if it doesn't work, well, at least it will keep you entertained until the hiccups stop naturally!

IT'S UNHEALTHY TO HOLD BACK A SNEEZE

HOW TRUE IS IT?
LET THAT SNEEZE RIP!

*J*ust by breathing, you inhale all kinds of dirt, dust, pollen, and other types of microscopic rubbish that float in the air. To clear this nastiness out of your nasal passages, nature developed the sneeze—and not just for humans. Mammals, birds, and even reptiles rely on the sneeze for a little sinus housekeeping.

We can't speak for the velocity of a parakeet's sneeze, but when a human sneezes, the microscopic dust flies at more than 100 feet (30 meters) per second. According to Hampton Sides, editor of *Outside* magazine's "The Wild File" column, the force of a human sneeze is on par with the force of a fire hose.

Trying to suppress a sneeze, then, is good manners run amok. You feel a sneeze coming on because your body has decided that it has reached its quotient of airborne gunk and the time to expel it is now. Besides, suppressing a sneeze truly can be very dangerous.

Sides reports that an unreleased sneeze has been known to cause "fractures in the nasal cartilage, major nosebleeds, burst eardrums, broken blood vessels in the eye, detached retinas, even fatal strokes." Sides goes on to say that if you happen to be ill when trying to clamp down on a sneeze, you could "drive millions of tiny pathogenic particles deep into the sinus tissues, which can lead to serious infections." But there is more. "Alternatively," Sides continues, "it can force air under the skin, causing a condition known as facial emphysema."

So for heaven's sake, the next time you feel a sneeze coming on, just let her rip!

WHAT HAPPENS WHEN WE SNEEZE?

Lots of things can set off a sneeze. Dust. Pollen. Cat or dog dander. Germs. Pepper. When you breathe in such gunk, the tiny hairs inside your nostrils trap it to keep it from being inhaled into your lungs. As these tiny particles tickle or irritate the inside of your nostrils, your nose transmits a message to what we might call "the sneeze center" of your brain to prepare to expel the unwanted irritant. At that point, the brain sends messages to the various muscle groups that must all work together to generate a sneeze.

The muscles of the abdomen, the chest, the diaphragm, the vocal chords, and the back of the throat all come into play when you sneeze. And there is one other group of muscles at work: the muscles of the eyelids. Every time you sneeze, your eyes close.

A Dog's Mouth is Cleaner Than a Human's

HOW TRUE IS IT?
THINK TWICE BEFORE
GIVING SPOT A KISS.

*I*t's a matter of faith among most kids (and plenty of adults) that a dog's mouth is so clean that a couple of licks from a pooch is as good as a few swabs of antiseptic.

Alas, the dog's-mouth-is-sterile myth is, indeed, a myth. Dr. Gary "Ask the Vet" Clemons says that "a dog's mouth contains a lot of bacteria." To emphasize his point, Dr. Clemons adds, "Remember, a dog's tongue is not only his washcloth but also his toilet paper."

Researchers at Stanford University found that on average the human mouth harbors 37 types of bacteria. Researchers at the University of Southern California found that a dog's mouth contains on average 53 types of bacteria.

The sterile dog's mouth old wives' tale goes hand-in-hand with another old wives' tale: that being bitten by a human is more dangerous, in terms of infection and other medical complications, than being bitten by some other animal. In fact, a 1988 study published in the *Annals of Emergency Medicine* found, "Human bites…do not seem to have any higher risk than animal bites, which have an infection rate of about 10%." The danger rate of human bites only goes up if the wound is left untreated.

As for dog bites, the Centers for Disease Control and Prevention reports that in the United States approximately 5 million humans are bitten by dogs every year, with emergency rooms seeing about 1,000 dog-bite victims per day. The number of dog bites is growing, too. Over a 10-year period in the United States, the number of dog bites increased by 37 percent—despite the fact that dog ownership increased by only 2 percent.

On average in the U.S.A. there are 17 dog-attack fatalities per year. Who are these dogs biting? Not burglars—that's another myth. The chances that your watchdog or house pet will attack and kill a burglar are very low—one in 177. There is a 70 percent chance, however, that the dog's victim will be a child. According to the *Journal of the American Medical Association*, 333,687 kids visit emergency rooms annually with dog-bite injuries, second only to baseball or softball injuries.

Also, folks who insist that a dog's mouth is sterile are forgetting that by biting, dogs transmit rabies, tetanus, Pasteurella, and other potentially lethal diseases. You might want to remember that the next time your dog jumps up to lick your face.

THE NOT-SO-STERILE BOXER

A 1996 article in the British medical journal *The Lancet* reported that a 31-year-old British man developed a painful mouth and throat infection known as Ludwig's angina after romping with a friend's boxer dog. Researchers at the Royal Hampshire County Hospital in Winchester, England, where the man was treated, concluded that the dog passed along the infection while licking the man's face.

Analysis of the man's blood revealed the presence of *Pasteurella multocida*, a bacterium found in the mouths of animals and birds. A saliva sample taken from the dog's mouth also contained *Pasteurella multocida* bacteria. The man recovered after being treated with penicillin.

VAMPIRE BATS SUCK HUMAN BLOOD

HOW TRUE IS IT?
ONLY ONCE IN A WHILE.

*H*umans have always found bats to be creepy. In the Bible's Book of Leviticus, God ranks bats among "unclean fowls" that Jews may not eat. Shakespeare's witches in *Macbeth* tossed a little "wool of bat" into their cauldron. And of course, once Bram Stoker's blood-chilling novel, *Dracula*, was published in 1897, any hope of rehabilitating the bat's reputation was finished.

The vampire bat is found in northern Mexico, Argentina, and Chile, and on the islands of Trinidad and Margarita off the coast of Venezuela. It does indeed survive on blood. Flying about 3 feet (1 meter) off the ground, it hunts for prey, which includes wild animals, cows, horses, pigs, and, occasionally, humans.

Bats find a victim by using a type of vampirish radio wave. Out of its nose the hungry bat emits an ultra-high-frequency sound. The sounds travels outward until it strikes a mammal, then bounces back to be picked up by the bat's ultra-sensitive ears. This enables the bat to zero in on its target.

Let's say that the bat has found a pig, curled up on the ground and sound asleep. The bat lands nearby and crawls or hops over to its prey. Heat sensors located in the bat's nose identify the capillaries where the blood lies close to the surface of the pig's skin.

With its tongue and teeth the bat cleans the area where it intends to feed, then takes a bite from its prey, and begins to lap up—not suck—the blood. A chemical in the bat's saliva keeps the pig's blood from clotting. Once the bat has drunk its fill of blood (about two tablespoons), it is too heavy to fly.

Like a drunk falling off a bar stool, the bat drops off its prey to hide in the underbrush until it has digested its meal. A vampire bat must feast on blood every two or three days, or it will die.

Although Dracula, in the novel and the movies, has linked vampire bats with Transylvania, Europeans did not discover these creatures until the 16th century. Vampire tales, on the other hand, began to surface in Eastern Europe during the Middle Ages. Vampire bats got their names because, like the legendary vampires who rose from the dead and sucked the blood of living human beings, they, too, drank blood.

Unlike the mythical creature for whom they are named, vampire bats, when they do decide to feed on humans, usually aim for an ankle or a toe, not the neck. Fatalities caused by vampire bites stem from rabies, not blood loss. Many vampire bats do indeed carry this deadly disease. And their numbers appear to be on the rise. In March 2004, 13 Brazilians died after being bitten by rabies-carrying vampire bats. Brazilian health ministry officials speculated that deforestation and the availability of more livestock may have led to changes in the vampire bats' migratory patterns and increased their populations, possibly causing them to become more aggressive.

These bloodthirsty creatures do pose a threat to people in Central and South America. According to the Smithsonian Institution, efforts to reduce the number of vampire bats in this area of the world began in 1968, when deaths among cattle bitten by rabid vampire bats became a serious economic threat. The old wives' tales about vampire bats' danger to human beings remain the stuff of medieval legend and Bram Stoker's imagination. But if you live in Central or South American, make sure you and your animals keep rabies vaccinations current.

WINE IS GOOD FOR YOU

HOW TRUE IS IT?
TRUE—AS LONG AS YOU'RE
ONLY DRINKING A GLASS OR
TWO A DAY.

Two thousand years ago St. Timothy, a disciple of St. Paul, suffered from chronic stomach trouble. In a letter to his young friend the great apostle broke off his instructions on how to run a church to offer a little medical advice. "Take a little wine," St. Paul wrote, "for thy stomach's sake." More recently there have been reports that the French and Italians have lower levels of cholesterol and suffer less from heart disease than their American cousins—this in spite of diets that are rich in cream, butter, and cheese—because they drink red wine every day. Other health benefits have been attributed to the fruit of the vine, but is there any scientific data to back it up? Happily, the answer is yes.

Researchers at Chicago's Northwestern University Medical School found that the stuff that does the trick is resveratrol, a form of estrogen that is concentrated in grape skins that produce red wine. Out in the vineyard, nature created resveratrol to protect grapes against fungal infections. In the lab, however, researchers have discovered that resveratrol also acts as an antioxidant and an anticoagulant. It also has been found to be toxic to prostate cancer cells, while leaving healthy cells unharmed. Meanwhile, in Spain, researchers at the Spanish Council for Scientific Research reported that if grapes are subjected to low levels of ultraviolet radiation before they are made into wine, the level of resveratrol will increase from one milligram in a glass of red wine to more than three milligrams. In other words, a little ultraviolet radiation is all it takes to deliver three times the health benefits in each glass of red wine.

But what if you prefer white wine? After all, the resveratrol-packed grape skins are removed from the vats in order to make white wine. No problem. Scientists in Israel have discovered a method to increase the level of resveratrol in white wine. By fermenting the whole squeezed grapes in alcohol for 18 hours before removing their skins, the antioxidants in the white wine were increased six times above their normal level. This method also boosted the amount of sugar in the white wine, creating something akin to a sweet dessert wine.

But wine is not just good for the body; it is also good for the brain, especially for those in the more creative professions. Six thousand British government employees were recruited for a study sponsored by the University of London. In a series of tests that measured memory, general intelligence, and mathematical and verbal skills, teetotalers scored the lowest. Those who drank just one alcoholic beverage a week did a little better, while those who drank a half-bottle of wine every day had the highest test scores.

Researchers found that the alcohol fired up the brain cells and made the wine-drinker more imaginative and more productive. Good news aside, because of the well-established detrimental effects of excessive alcohol consumption on the body, the old wives—and doctors—advise everyone to drink in moderation.

APPLYING VINEGAR RELIEVES WASP STINGS

HOW TRUE IS IT?
THIS REMEDY COMES WITH
A STING IN THE TALE...

*T*he old wives are a great source of remedies for minor ailments such as bee and wasp stings. They maintain that wasp stings are alkaline, so should be neutralized with vinegar, while bee stings are acidic so can be alleviated with a paste of bicarbonate of soda with water.

Is there any truth to this store-cupboard wisdom? Well, a little. Wasp stings are indeed slightly alkaline, and bee venom contains formic acid, although this is not the single active ingredient that causes the pain of the sting. However, the traditional remedies are unlikely to be effective because the venom from the stings is injected under the skin and after a few minutes spreads deep into the tissues. Applying solutions to the skin surface is unlikely to get near the venom to neutralize it.

For a more effective remedy, first wash the site of the sting with water to try to prevent the venom from spreading. Then apply an antihistamine cream or take an oral antihistamine.

The greatest risk from wasp and bee stings occurs if you're allergic to them. Symptoms of allergic reaction may include difficulty in breathing, dizziness and nausea, and extreme tiredness. Seek medical attention immediately if you experience these symptoms. Another, less serious, risk is that the site of the sting may become infected with bacteria carried by the insects. If your sting is still hot and inflamed after 8–12 hours, you may need antibiotics to treat the infection.

MEN HAVE ONE LESS RIB THAN WOMEN

HOW TRUE IS IT?
THIS TALE COMES
UP SHORT.

*I*n the Book of Genesis we read that after God had made Adam from clay, he said, "It is not good for man to be alone; let us make him a help like unto himself." So God cast a deep sleep upon Adam, removed one of Adam's ribs, then filled up the empty space in the rib cage with flesh. From this rib he made Eve. Ever since, men have had one less rib than women.

Of course, the Bible does not say that all Adam's male descendants would be a rib short, but that hasn't stopped the old wives. So in 2004, Dallas, Texas's premier rib joint, Tony Roma's restaurant, conducted a survey among the rib-savvy members of its Loyalty Club to see how many people believed the men-are-one-rib-short story. Out of 9,428 respondents (men and women) 47 percent thought the story was true.

To settle the issue, Tony Roma's contacted Dr. Stephen Sapp, professor and chairman of the Department of Religious Studies at the University of Miami. Dr. Sapp explained that the removal of a bone, miraculously or surgically, does not cause a change in a person's genetic makeup that he would pass along to his offspring. To clarify the point, he made an analogy: to believe that because Adam lost a rib all his male descendants are a rib short is like believing that if you have your appendix removed, all your descendants will be born without an appendix.

In case you are wondering, the human body has 12 pairs of ribs. That's standard equipment for both men and women.

LEMMINGS COMMIT MASS SUICIDE

HOW TRUE IS IT?
YOU CAN'T BE SERIOUS.

Since 1958, old wives have been stating with absolute certainty that, periodically, lemmings commit mass suicide by running to the edge of a cliff and hurling themselves into the sea. It's an indisputable fact. After all, they saw it in a movie called *White Wilderness*, part of the Disney studio's True Life Adventure series. The scene of the little critters jumping off the cliff was so vivid that even the *American Heritage Dictionary* defines a lemming as a rodent "noted for its mass migrations into the sea."

Disney and the dictionary—can you get two more reliable sources than that? Well, yes, you can. The Canadian Broadcasting Corporation, for one.

In 1983, CBC producer Brian Vallee, tipped off by wildlife biologists that lemmings do not possess a self-destruct gene, began to investigate the Disney film. Vallee found that the mass suicide scene was faked. The Disney filmmakers bought a few dozen lemmings from Inuits in Manitoba; by using tight camera angles they created the impression of a horde of hysterical lemmings running across a snow-covered landscape toward their doom.

The film does show lemmings falling through the air and drowning in the water. However, those scenes were faked, too. The movie was made in Alberta, a land-locked province of Canada. So the filmmakers chose for their location a cliff above a river. Again, tight camera angles enabled them to create the impression that the river was actually the ocean.

As for the hurling part—it was members of the film crew who threw the animals off the cliff.

It's a damning story, but Alaska state wildlife biologist Thomas McDonough is willing to cut Disney a little slack. "Disney had to have gotten that idea from somewhere," he says. And McDonough believes he knows the source: Disney mistook the lemmings' habit of mass dispersal for self-destruction.

Lemmings are small rodents, related to voles. Their population in the wild fluctuates depending on predators and food supply. If they find themselves in a place with few predators and lots to eat, a lemming population can increase in size ten times in just one year. Once the food supply is gone, however, the lemmings disperse en masse to look for a new habitat. (By the way, moose and beaver do the same thing.)

Zoologist Gordon Jarrell, an expert in small mammals with the University of Alaska Fairbanks, says that in Scandinavia hordes of lemmings have been observed backed up at a river or some other body of water. Lemmings can swim, but in such a pile-up quite a few lemmings will drown. That appears to be the source of the myth and the movie.

IT'S BAD LUCK TO BUY A HOUSE WHERE A MURDER TOOK PLACE

HOW TRUE IS IT?
NOT AT ALL.

*T*he chic condominium where Nicole Brown Simpson and Ron Goldman were murdered sat on the market for over two years before it found a buyer. The highly desirable Brentwood address, the 3,400 square feet of living space, the four bedrooms, three bathrooms, and rooftop patio—none of these could overcome the taint of the double murder. When the condo finally did sell, it was at a price far lower than one would expect for a comparable home in Brentwood.

Randall Bell of Bell & Associates in Laguna Niguel, California, has made selling stigmatized properties his specialty. He says that real-estate agents should expect to discount houses that were a notorious crime scene by as much as 25 percent. In time, Bell says, the stigma goes away, "but it takes 10 to 25 years."

In other words, houses where murders have taken place mean less money for real-estate agents and homeowners. But those in the market for a house may be passing up a real bargain if they let superstition get in the way of common sense.

Ghosts and Satan, as *The Skeptic's Dictionary* points out, could change addresses any time if they truly had the powers old wives' tales say they do. So why would they stay in one place for centuries, particularly one where bad things happened to them? Older homes provide especially fertile ground for so-called paranormal activity. But eerie sounds occur, in part, when air passes through walls—even in a new building. Cracks and crevices, normal signs of wear and tear (or of bad builders) make room for drafts to seep in, not ghosts. And instruments designed to pick up the electromagnetic fields poltergeists allegedly give off work because of natural, not supernatural, phenomena. Most objects possess enough electromagnetic radiation to set the needles of these devices in motion.

However, anyone saddled with stigmatized property can take some comfort from knowing some people actually want to buy so-called haunted houses. Many like the prestige and excitement a ghostly inhabitant brings to their lives.

TIPS FOR SELLING CRIME SCENE HOUSES

Real estate agent Randall Bell suggests three simple steps for getting a tainted property off the market.

1. Always tell a potential buyer that a crime took place in the house. Real estate agents can be taken to court if they fail to disclose such information.

2. Try to rent the house. Immediately after the killing, no buyer will touch the place. But having tenants in the house for few years will help diminish its notoriety.

3. Renovate the property. Make it look different than it did on the day of the crime. Repaint. Change the appearance of the front door. Chop down existing trees, or plant new ones. Tear down an existing fence, or build a privacy wall.

Remember that the house has been seen on television and in newspapers across the country (and possibly around the world). Make changes so it is not instantly recognizable as "that house."

COLD HANDS, WARM HEART

HOW TRUE IS IT?
IT'S THE TRUTH,
HANDS-DOWN.

olklore assures us that women with cold hands have very warm hearts. Though there haven't been any studies showing a correlation between body temperature and a predisposition toward kindness, the literal interpretation of the assertion has been investigated. And according to the latest scientific evidence, the old wives got it right.

At the University of Utah Dr. Joseph Lyon and his team of graduate students recruited 219 individuals—141 females and 78 males—ranging in age from infants to seniors in their eighties, for this unusual experiment.

The research began as a hunch. Lyon was working at an urgent-care facility when he thought he felt a pattern in patient skin temperature: women felt cooler to the touch than men. As an early test of his intuition, Lyon measured a nurse's skin temperature and then measured his own. The nurse's temperature came in at 75 degrees Fahrenheit (24 Celsius); Lyon's registered 95 degrees Fahrenheit (35 Celsius).

Soon Lyon and his graduate students were collecting volunteers and taking readings of the temperature of the fingernails of their subjects' left and right middle fingers. To record their measurements, the research team used ultrasensitive infrared tympanic thermometers. The results found that on average a woman's hands are 2.8 degrees Fahrenheit (1.55 Celsius) cooler than a man's hands. But, short of surgery, how do you measure the warmth of a human heart?

That's when the muse visited Lyon and his students for the second time: they realized that they could establish the core body temperature of every volunteer in the study by measuring both their eardrums.

The result: on average the women's hearts tested at 97.8 degrees Fahrenheit (36 Celsius) while the hearts of men averaged a cooler 97.4 degrees Fahrenheit (36 Celsius).

At first glance the whole project sounds like a lark, but Dr. Lyon believes that the cold hands, warm heart experiment could lead to useful medical information. He and his team are planning to study whether people with cold hands have more trouble with arthritis and cardiovascular disease.

PEOPLE WITH RED HAIR ARE TEMPERAMENTAL

HOW TRUE IS IT?
JUST A STEREOTYPE.

ou don't want to be a redhead in France. It's enough that red hair is taken as a sign of a short fuse and a sexually voracious appetite, but French old wives' tales insist that people with red hair are not to be trusted. The stigma is so widespread that redheaded French women have banded together to form an advocacy group known as Association Francaise des Rousses.

Red hair is the result of a recessive gene that tends to occur in people from Western Europe. Between 3 and 5 percent of Western Europeans and their descendants around the globe are redheads. That number rises to about 15 percent in certain Irish and Scottish towns that 1,200 years ago experienced frequent visits from the Vikings. Different cultures have different takes on redheads. In Denmark a redheaded child is considered a blessing. In Corsica, you want to ward off a redhead just as you want to ward off the evil eye, while in Poland it's said that if you pass three redheads in the street, it's a sign that you will win the state lottery.

According to Harvard dermatologist Madhu Pathak, redheads have several strikes against them. Redheads tend to have fair skin, so they haven't enough pigment to filter out sunlight. This makes them more susceptible to sunburn, and skin cancer.

But the rest is fable: no study has ever proven that redheads have hotter tempers, or libidos, than anyone else.

IT CAN BE TOO COLD TO SNOW

HOW TRUE IS IT?
IT'S THE COLD, HARD
TRUTH.

*A*t first glance, the old saying, "It's too cold to snow," seems idiotic. It would be like saying that your freezer is too cold to make ice. Come on, the only time it snows is when it's cold, right?

Actually, no. In this case the old wives who specialize in weather folklore know what they are talking about. Matt Peroutka, a meteorologist at the National Weather Service's Techniques Development Laboratory in Silver Spring, Maryland, explains, "The atmosphere must contain moisture to generate snow, and very cold air contains very little moisture. Once the air temperature at ground level drops below about −10 degrees Fahrenheit (−20 degrees Celsius), snowfall becomes unlikely in most places."

The temperature must be below freezing for ice crystals to attach to each other and drift down to earth. But when the temperatures are extremely, insanely low, the ice crystals do not hook up. There can be precipitation under extremely cold conditions, but it isn't considered snow. The common name for the stuff falling from the sky on a brutally cold day is ice needles. It happens pretty often in the Arctic, where such precipitation is called an ice fog.

SHAVE YOUR BODY HAIR AND IT GROWS BACK THICKER

HOW TRUE IS IT?
NOT AT ALL.

Swimmers and bodybuilders have long shaved their bodies. These days many ordinary guys remove their body hair so the world can enjoy an unobstructed view of their gym-built muscles. According to the old wives, however, once you shave your body, the hair will grow back thicker and maybe even darker than it was originally.

It sounds ominous. Or at least ironic. But it's not true. There are issues to consider before shaving your body, but the fear of being transformed from a masculine, moderately hairy guy into a shaggy gorilla is not among them.

The most common condition associated with shaving body hair is razor burn, a red, itchy skin irritation that is generally caused by dragging the razor too hard across the skin, or shaving the hairs against the grain. In some cases a razor can even infect the hair follicles. The act of shaving opens the follicles, making them susceptible to bacteria. Infected follicles, a condition known as folliculitis, produce red bumps on the skin, which are both uncomfortable and unsightly. Generally an antibacterial soap will clear up the problem, but a more serious case in which the follicles fill up with pus requires a trip to the doctor.

There are many other hair-related myths. For example, the old wives assure us that brushing your hair 100 times before going to bed will make it thick and lustrous. This is nonsense. Excessive brushing can actually break healthy strands of hair, scratch your scalp, and pull out hair that your head wasn't yet ready to shed.

What about the claim that if you pull out one gray hair, two or more will grow in its place? It makes sense—but only if you believe in vengeful gray-hair gods. In fact, this myth is rooted in a misconception about how hair grows. First, in most cases gray hair is a sign that you are aging. Once you pluck out a hair, it takes six months for a new one to fully grow in. By the time the plucked-out hair's replacement grows in, you're six months older, and chances are that you've acquired a few more gray hairs than you had on the day you performed the plucking.

The ubiquitous strands of hair curled up in just about everybody's shower drains have given birth to the notion that shampooing makes hair fall out. It simply isn't true. Shampooing has no effect on healthy hair. Our heads are sloughing off old dead hair all the time. The strands of hair that have collected in and around your drain were ready to drop off anyway—the act of washing just eased their passage.

Cosmetic companies have told us that we shouldn't trim off split ends, rather we should heal them by buying their miracle split-end restorative products. Baloney. Split ends can't be healed. They can be temporarily fused together by some kind of commercial goop. But once the goop is washed away, the split ends will reappear.

FRIDAY THE THIRTEENTH IS UNLUCKY

HOW TRUE IS IT?
WELL, IT'S CERTAINLY
BAD FOR BUSINESS.

Whenever Friday the 13th rolls around on the calendar, you can count on virtually every radio and television newscaster to make some reference to it. It is the gold standard of old wives' tales, and perhaps their most successful (in terms of being one of the most widely held phobias).

Where does it come from? It is actually an alliance of two separate terrors common in the Western world: fear of the number 13, and fear of Friday. Put these two together and you have very potent negative juju.

One reason for fear of 13 comes from the New Testament. There were 13 guests at the Last Supper, one of whom, Judas Iscariot, left the meal early to betray Jesus. As a corollary, this is the origin of the superstition that having 13 at a table is bad luck.

Thomas Fernsler of the Mathematics and Science Education Resource Center at the University of Delaware explains that in almost all Western societies, 12 is regarded as a complete number. An even dozen is as good as it gets: 12 months in a year, 12 signs of the zodiac, 12 gods of Olympus, 12 tribes of Israel, and 12 apostles of Jesus. Add one more, and that once-tidy dozen is suddenly off-kilter.

Donald Dossey, founder of the Stress Management Center and Phobia Institute in Asheville, North Carolina, reports that fear of the number 13 shows up in places we wouldn't expect. More than 80 percent of high-rises lack a 13th floor. Many airports don't have a Gate 13. Rare is the hospital or hotel with a Room 13.

So that accounts for the 13 part of this equation. As for the Friday part, its roots go back to the Bible, especially Good Friday, when Jesus Christ was crucified. Adam and Eve were expelled from the Garden of Eden on a Friday. Cain slew his brother Abel on a Friday. God cursed the builders of the Tower of Babel on a Friday. Noah's Flood began on a Friday. And Solomon's Temple was destroyed by the Babylonians on a Friday. Ever since, superstitious people have regarded Friday with suspicion.

However, Friday the 13th is only truly bad news in the business community. Dossey says, "It's been estimated that $800 or $900 million is lost in business on this day because people will not fly or do business they would normally do." How can a myth cause so much money to be lost? Because, Dossey goes on to explain, between 17 and 21 million people just in the United States have a superstitious dread of Friday the 13th. They may reshuffle their schedule so no major decisions must be made on that day, they may call in sick, or they may succumb to a full-blown incapacitating panic attack.

And it's not just business that shows the effects of Friday the 13th phobia. In England on Friday the 13th, the number of people admitted to hospitals because of car accidents has been shown to rise about 52 percent, perhaps because so many drivers and pedestrians are on edge that day.

Richard Wiseman, a psychologist at the University of Hertfordshire in Hatfield, England, believes that the bad luck associated with Friday the 13th is a self-fulfilling prophecy. People who think of themselves as unlucky tend to be very nervous on Friday the 13th and therefore much more prone to accidents. Which, of course, just reinforces their belief that they are unlucky and Friday the 13th is their personal day of disaster.

DON'T EAT OYSTERS IF THERE'S NOT AN "R" IN THE MONTH

HOW TRUE IS IT?
IT IS—OR SO THE OYSTERS
WOULD HAVE US BELIEVE...

*T*he English have always been wild about oysters. Even Englishmen who lived miles away from the coast managed to get their hands on the tasty bivalves, as witnessed by the huge deposits of oyster shells archeologists have uncovered in 2,000-year-old dumps along Hadrian's Wall on the English–Scotch border.

Wherever the English went, they took their love of oysters with them. The Pilgrims in Massachusetts were delighted to find oyster beds just steps away from their cabins. The English also took with them this bit of oyster lore: only eat oysters during months that have an "r" in them; anyone who slurps down an oyster during May, June, July, or August is just asking for trouble.

There is something to this. For all those centuries before refrigeration, shellfish spoiled quickly during the summer months. And there was another reason to leave oysters alone during the summer: it is the period when oysters spawn. According to the proprietors of the Golden Point Oyster Sea Farm in Maine, spawning takes a lot out of the oyster, leaving the meat tasting "watery, runny, lacking flavor, and generally not worth eating."

It's best to wait "until they recover a bit by feeding for a month or two." In other words, wait until September—an "r" month. Today, of course, refrigeration is not a concern. The only reason not to eat oysters during the summer is a matter of taste.

OPOSSUMS PLAY DEAD TO FOOL PREDATORS

HOW TRUE IS IT?
100 PERCENT TRUE.

To "play possum" is an American colloquialism for pretending to be dead. Old wives tell lots of stories about animal behavior, so how about this one? Do opossums really play dead so that a predator will leave them alone?

The answer is yes. If you were to grab an opossum, you'd see the critter go catatonic instantly and assume the road-kill position: body curled, eyes blank, little claws turned inward like a half-formed fist. For the sake of realism, the "dead" possum drools from its mouth and releases foul green fluid from its anal glands. It's not only looks dead, it's disgusting to be around.

The act is absolutely convincing. Alfred L. Gardiner, curator of mammals for the National Biological Survey says, "You can freely handle [catatonic opossums], and even touch their eyeballs, and there's no reflex whatsoever." Gardiner goes on to say that in this state the opossum will not even respond to pain.

By some quirk of nature, opossums don't play dead when a predator is coming; instead, they wait until they are caught. By putting on a mighty convincing imitation of carrion (the stinky green slime oozing out the rear is a nice touch), the opossum manages to convince more than a few carnivores that he is not worth eating—and may even be dangerous to consume. The number of mauled but still alive opossums that possum-watchers have seen in the wild suggests that the tactic works.

SLEEPING IN BLUE SHEETS MAKES A GROOM VIRILE

HOW TRUE IS IT?
TRUE BLUE? PERHAPS MORE THAN YOU MIGHT THINK.

*I*n some parts of Mexico the old wives insist that on their wedding night the happy couple should bed down in a set of blue sheets. The color is said to make the groom virile. Can something as apparently random as the color of bed linen actually influence a new husband's performance? Maybe.

Marketing research firms found that consumers make up their minds about a product or a setting in less than 90 seconds. According to these researchers, consumers base anywhere between 62 percent and 90 percent of their judgment on color. For example, Pantone, the company that printers and designers use for the widest array of ink colors, has known for decades that the most effective posters, flyers and advertisements are printed in black type on yellow background. Tests have shown that this color combination gets the highest scores for legibility, attracting the eye, and sticking in the memory.

Then there is this unexpected bit of medical research from Washington State University: patients have a higher tolerance for pain, and recover more quickly using less prescription medication, when they recuperate in a room painted green or in a room that contains lots of green accents such as plants.

Have you noticed how many fast-food restaurants are decorated in a color scheme of reds, yellows, and oranges? There is a reason for it: color research has shown that such "hot" colors somehow prompt people to eat more quickly. Restaurants decorated in blues and greens encourage more leisurely dining.

Many jails have holding cells painted a shade known as Baker-Miller Pink (popularly known as Drunk Tank Pink). It is a shade that comes close to the color of bubble gum. Why such a color in a jail, of all places? Dr. Alexander Schauss, director of the American Institute for Biosocial Research in Tacoma, Washington, discovered that this shade of pink has a positive effect on angry and violent prisoners. "It's a tranquilizing color," Dr. Schauss said.

So what about blue sheets? Color researchers have found that blue can decrease the heart rate and have a calming effect. And a bridegroom who is calm and confident rather than tense and over-eager is likely to perform better.

POTATOES WITH A GREENISH TINGE ARE POISONOUS

HOW TRUE IS IT?
TRUE, BUT WHEN IT COMES TO POISON CONTENT, WE'RE TALKING SMALL POTATOES.

*B*ack in the 16th century, when the white potato first found its way from South America to Europe, it was not immediately popular. In England, Queen Elizabeth I's cook threw out the potato, cooked the greens of the potato vine, and served them to Her Majesty. Elizabeth did not like the result. Still, the potato hung around in England, although only as an ornamental plant in English gardens.

While the English wrote off the potato as unpalatable, it developed a much worse reputation in other parts of the globe. French farmers believed eating a potato would cause leprosy. And colonists in America thought white potatoes were poisonous.

These old suspicions regarding the nutritious, delicious potato may be the source for the old wives' tale that potatoes that show a touch a green under their skin are toxic.

Potatoes, of course, grow underground and are happiest when they remain in the dark. These days potatoes move from the field to the supermarket, where they spend days under the glare of artificial light. It is the constant exposure to light that produces the greenish color under the potato's skin. This green color is solanine. Yes, solanine is toxic, but according to *Science Daily*, you would have to ingest 200 milligrams of solanine in order to give yourself a lethal dose of green-potato poison. Although a completely green potato could be packing 200 milligrams of solanine, it is unlikely that anyone would choose to eat it.

FUN FACTS ABOUT POTATOES

- Archeological evidence tells us that the Incas of Peru were cultivating potatoes by 200 B.C.

- The potato came to Europe via the Spanish conquistadores who encountered it in the Andes of South America in 1537.

- The average American eats about 140 pounds (63 kilograms) of potatoes. The average European consumes about 280 pounds (127 kilograms) of potatoes per year.

- The record for peeling the most potatoes using standard kitchen knives was set on March 17, 1981, at the Bourke Street Hall in Melbourne, Australia. The winner peeled 587 pounds, 8 ounces (266.5 kilograms) of potatoes in 45 minutes.

Generally the green tint is limited to the potato skin. Simply cut it off and cook the potato as you usually would.

A Severed Head Stays Alive
for Several Minutes

HOW TRUE IS IT?
WELL...

*D*octor Joseph-Ignace Guillotin is often credited with designing the sleek, efficient gadget that decapitated King Louis XVI, Queen Marie Antoinette, and thousands of less distinguished victims during the French Revolution's Reign of Terror. He intended it as a swift, tidy, and humane form of execution. Compared to the unspeakable agonies of being burned alive at the stake, or having one's bones smashed while bound to a wheel, the guillotine was a genuinely merciful step forward.

Soon after the guillotine was in regular operation, executioners and others on the scaffold began to notice that the severed heads often seemed to still be "alive." The eyes opened or twitched. The lips trembled, or the mouth opened as if the victim were trying to speak.

The most famous case is that of Charlotte Corday, the young woman who stabbed to death the French revolutionary Marat while he soaked in his bath tub. After she was guillotined, the executioner lifted her head out of the basket and displayed it to the crowd as he slapped its face. Corday's cheeks reddened and her face took on an angry expression. The old wives said that the guillotine worked so swiftly that for several minutes after the head was separated from the body it remained alive and conscious. The idea was terribly unsettling, to say the least.

This notion hung on so long that in 1905 a French physician named Beaurieux decided to settle the matter by studying the head of a criminal named Languille who was scheduled to be guillotined at 5:30 a.m. on June 28, 1905.

After the blade of the guillotine fell, Dr. Beaurieux observed, "The eyelids and lips of the guillotined man worked in irregularly rhythmic contractions for about five or six seconds." Beaurieux waited a few seconds more until he saw the muscles of the face relax and the eyelids half close, then called the man's name.

"I saw the eyelids slowly lift up, without any spasmodic contractions—I insist advisedly on this peculiarity—but with an even movement, quite distinct and normal, such as happens in everyday life, with people awakened or torn from their thoughts...Languille's eyes definitely fixed themselves on mine and the pupils focused themselves. I was not, then, dealing with the sort of vague dull look without any expression, that can be observed any day in dying people to whom one speaks: I was dealing with undeniably living eyes which were looking at me."

After several seconds, the eyelids closed again. Once again the doctor called out his name. "Once more, without any spasm, slowly, the eyelids lifted and undeniably living eyes fixed themselves on mine with perhaps even more penetration than the first time." The eyelids closed again, and when Beaurieux called Languille's name for the third time there was no reaction. He lifted the lids with his fingers and saw that the eyes had taken on "the glazed look which they have in death." According to Dr. Beaurieux, the whole scene took about 25 to 30 seconds.

Languille may have remained conscious for a few seconds after being beheaded. However, his remaining conscious for 25 to 30 seconds seems unlikely. When the head is severed from the body, both parts quickly lose enormous amounts of blood. Blood loss leads—in rapid succession—to a massive drop in blood pressure, oxygen deprivation (cerebral hypoxia, as doctors call it), unconsciousness, and brain death.

SEVEN IS THE PERFECT NUMBER

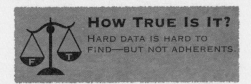

HOW TRUE IS IT?
HARD DATA IS HARD TO
FIND—BUT NOT ADHERENTS.

*A*mong Jews and Christians, Egyptians and Greeks, seafarers and motivational speakers, seven is the perfect number. It was the Pythagoreans, the disciples of the ancient Greek mathematician Pythagoras, who first applauded the perfection of seven because it was the sum of 3, which represents the triangle, and 4, which represents the square. And among the Pythagoreans, the triangle and the square were the two perfect geometrical forms.

Other ancient civilizations regarded seven as the number of perfection. The Babylonians believed the seven planets were arranged in levels on spheres of crystal, with the seventh planet existing on the highest level known as "seventh heaven"—an expression we still use for being in a place that couldn't possibly be any better. In the ruins of ancient Nineveh the archeologist A.H. Layard (1817–1894) found clay tablets covered with charms, prayers, and incantations that were supposed to be recited seven times in order to work.

Groups of seven occur at least 300 times in the Bible, one of the most famous being the formula that brought down the walls of Jericho. For seven days, seven priests walked before the Ark of the Covenant, blowing seven ram's horns. On the seventh day they circled Jericho seven times. On the seventh circuit they blew their horns and the walls came tumbling down. And in ancient Ireland, a man was considered well-to-do if he possessed these seven things: a house, a mill, a kiln, a barn, a sheep pen, a shed for calves, and a pigsty.

No matter where you look in high culture or popular culture, you run into sevens. The Seven Days of the Week. The Seven Days of Creation. Seven Fat Years and Seven Lean Years. The Seven Gods of Egypt. The Seven Horses of Mithra. The Seven Wonders of the World. The Seven Wise Men of Greece. The Seven Hills of Rome. The Seven-Branched Menorah. The Seven Lucky Gods of Japan. The Seven Archangels. The Seven Sleepers of Ephesus. Seventh Heaven. The Seven Deadly Sins. The Seven Cardinal Virtues. The Seven Sorrows of the Virgin Mary. The Seven Chakras. The Seven Ancient Planets. The Seven Sisters Constellation. The Seven Seas. The Seven Ages of Man. The Seven Cities of Cibola. The Seven Colors of the Rainbow. The Amish Dinner of Seven Sweets and Seven Sours. *The Seven-Year Itch.* The Seven Dwarves. *Seven Brides for Seven Brothers. The Seven Samurai. The Magnificent Seven.* Trial of the Chicago Seven. T.E. Lawrence's *The Seven Pillars of Wisdom.* Stephen Covey's *7 Habits of Highly Effective People.*

You get the idea.

The Pythagorean rationale for why seven should be such a great number makes sense, but why it is regarded as an ideal number in virtually every corner of the world and in virtually every period of history remains impossible to pin down. It is enough to recognize that the appeal of the number seven is rooted deep in the human psyche, and who are we to question Nature?

WHITE SPOTS ON YOUR NAILS MEAN YOU NEED CALCIUM

HOW TRUE IS IT?
IT'S MORE LIKELY YOU'RE
CLUMSY.

*T*he old wives are right in one respect: fingernails do offer clues about health problems, but low calcium is not one of them. According to food folklore, white spots on the fingernails mean that your diet is deficient in calcium. In fact those white spots are a sign that the nail has suffered some kind of minor injury, such as a bump or a bruise. It's not serious, and the white spots will disappear as the nail grows out.

But keep an eye on your fingernails for signs of more serious trouble. Dr. Louise Martin, a dermatologist at Providence Hospital in Rhode Island, explains how to recognize what your fingernails are telling you. Brittle or slow-growing nails are a sign that the nails are dehydrated, a common complaint among people who wear artificial nails or who spend a lot of time in water, such as swimmers. The solution is to apply a heavy moisturizer such as petroleum jelly at night before going to bed.

A dark brown or black streak on one fingernail could be a sign of cancer. Nails with a bluish tinge may be a sign of lung trouble. Nails that are turning yellow may indicate liver problems. In addition to color, the shape of the nails offers clues. Club nails, or nails that curl down around the tip of your fingers, can be a warning sign of lung or heart disease. Little dimples in your nails may be the result of a skin condition such as psoriasis.

But don't try to self-diagnose yourself from your fingernails. If you notice something out of the ordinary, go to a doctor.

A Cat Aboard Ship Brings Good Luck

HOW TRUE IS IT?
THE CAT DOES HAVE
ITS USES.

Sailors are said to be the most superstitious people on the planet. Given the danger and unpredictability of the sea, it's no wonder that sailors have so many beliefs and routines to ensure a safe voyage. While many of these nautical superstitions are questionable, the cat aboard ship at least has a practical purpose: it is nature's own exterminator of mice and rats.

But sailors have attributed other powers to the cat. If the ship's cat cried, the voyage would be rough. If the ship's cat was playful, the voyage would be successful, with good winds. If a cat walked toward a sailor, it meant good luck would come to him; if the cat started to approach the sailor then suddenly turned away, it meant the sailor could expect bad luck.

Some sailors believed that a cat possessed awesome powers. Make the ship's cat angry and it would raise a storm at sea by lashing its tail about. Although a cat's tail can't influence the weather, it is true that cats are sensitive to low atmospheric pressure systems that produce stormy weather. If a ship's cat seems restless, there's a good chance a storm is brewing.

It's thought that cats were first domesticated in Egypt 4,000 years ago to defend the country's grain supply against rodents. The first domesticated cats probably arrived in Europe around 900 B.C. aboard the ships of Phoenician traders. Since then ships have carried the cat to every corner of the world.

CHOCOLATE CAUSES ACNE

HOW TRUE IS IT?
CHOCOHOLICS REJOICE
—IT'S NOT TRUE.

s if high school weren't bad enough, that wretched period is when acne pops up on the face of virtually every teenager. It's Mother Nature's little joke: at the precise moment when kids are most self-conscious about their appearance, their faces become a minefield of pimples.

Trying to figure out how to make acne go away probably occupies as much of the adolescent mind as trying to figure out how to get a date. As we have seen, desperation is fertile ground for old wives' tales. The most widespread and persistent myth blames chocolate for bringing on acne. But that myth was exploded decades ago.

In 1969 medical researchers at the University of Pennsylvania School of Medicine recruited 65 volunteers who suffered from moderate acne. The doctors divided the subjects into two groups: one group ate candy bars packed with 10 times the usual amount of chocolate; the other group ate candy bars with no chocolate in them at all. At the end of four weeks, the volunteers who had eaten mega-amounts of chocolate showed no signs of increased acne.

So if it isn't chocolate, what does cause acne? Acne flares up when the pores of the skin become blocked. Each pore is an opening to a follicle, a tiny canal with an oil gland. When everything is working normally, the oil gland flushes out the follicle, washing away old skin cells and keeping the skin moisturized. If the glands produce too much oil, the pores become blocked and produce a lump on the skin commonly called a pimple.

Infants have been known to have acne, and some people are still struggling with it in their 30s and 40s and beyond. But for most people, the curse comes upon them in adolescence. Blame it on hormones. With the onset of puberty, boys and girls produce a bumper crop of hormones called androgens. One of the things androgens do is cause the oil glands beneath the skin to enlarge and generate more oil. As we said earlier, excess oil tends to clog up the pores.

Other factors can make acne worse. Cosmetics, especially oil-based products, can block the pores. Drugs such as steroids, testosterone, and estrogen can cause acne. For young women, changes in the hormonal level leading up to the menstrual period can cause a flare-up. Even genetics plays a role. Kids whose parents had bad bouts of acne will probably have the same trouble, too.

You can reduce acne to an extent by avoiding greasy makeup and oily skin lotions, using water-based products instead. And wash your face with a mild, non-abrasive soap. If the acne persists, a dermatologist can suggest a variety of treatments to clear it up. But giving up chocolate won't be one of them.

WE USE ONLY TEN PERCENT OF OUR BRAINS

HOW TRUE IS IT?
THINK AGAIN.

*I*f ever there was an old wives' tale with mass appeal, it is this one. Who could resist the notion that 90 percent of our brain is lying fallow, that we have the potential to leave Einstein in our intellectual dust?

If only it were true. Dr. Eric H. Chuder of the University of Washington's Department of Anesthesiology states, "I have not been able to track down the exact source of this myth, and I have never seen any scientific data to support it." Dr. Chuder is hardly alone. Barry L. Beyerstein of the Brain Behavior Laboratory at Simon Fraser University in Vancouver, Canada, points out the basic flaws in this old wives' tale. "First of all, it is obvious that the brain, like all our other organs, has been shaped by natural selection." Furthermore, brain tissue is, as Beyerstein puts it, "metabolically expensive both to grow and to run." It boggles the mind to imagine that nature would have permitted the brain to develop into a massively underemployed organ.

Both Chuder and Beyerstein agree: we use 100% of our gray matter, though not necessarily all at once. Benjamin Radford, psychologist and editor of *The Skeptical Inquirer*, observes, "Just as people don't use all of their muscle groups at one time, they also don't use all of their brain at once."

If the common-sense argument doesn't convince you, there is always the research of clinical neurologists. They have found that there are no spare brain parts just waiting to take over when other parts stop working due to a stroke or serious head injury. No part of the brain is immune to trauma, and no part is redundant. In the course of brain surgery, neurologists have directed electrical stimulation to every part of the brain. They did not find any areas that were dormant, just waiting for a chance to kick into high intellectual gear.

So where did this old wives' tale come from? Beyerstein thinks the late 19th/early 20th-century psychologist and philosopher William James (brother of the novelist Henry James) inadvertently popularized the 10 percent myth. Between his scholarly activities as a Harvard professor, James wrote articles for popular magazines urging readers to improve themselves.

A common theme in these articles was that individuals rarely realize more than a small percentage of their real potential. James never mentioned a particular percentage, but the self-help, power-of-positive-thinking, motivational speakers who followed him began to claim that we were only using 10 percent of our potential. It was easy for such a claim to be restated as "10 percent of our brain." Finally, in his preface to the 1936 edition of Dale Carnegie's self-help blockbuster, *How to Win Friends and Influence People*, the celebrity journalist Lowell Thomas brought the claim full circle by attributing the "we're only using 10 percent of our brain" myth to William James. "The 10-percent myth has undoubtedly motivated many people to strive for greater creativity and productivity in their lives," Beyerstein says. "Hardly a bad thing." But like so many old wives' tales, it is just too good to be true.

STICK YOUR TONGUE OUT AND YOU ABSORB MILLIONS OF GERMS

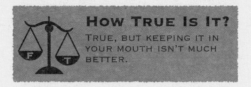

HOW TRUE IS IT?
TRUE, BUT KEEPING IT IN YOUR MOUTH ISN'T MUCH BETTER.

*T*here is a kernel of truth to the old wives' tale that cautions us not to stick out our tongues lest millions of germs collect there. The tongue does attract bacteria, but not because you were so rude as to stick it out of your mouth.

The bacteria on your tongue are called anaerobic, which means that they live in a mostly oxygen-free environment—your mouth. Floating around in there are dead cells from the lining of your mouth as well as tiny food particles. The anaerobic bacteria break these things down from solids into gases that smell pretty bad. The formal name for these gases is "volatile sulphur compounds," or VSC. Stand in front of a mirror and open your mouth. See that white stuff at the back of your tongue? That is VSC. The gases often get caught amid the tiny lumps and minuscule crevices of your tongue's taste-buds, where they become concentrated, resulting in bad breath, or halitosis, to use the clinical term.

To get rid of the bad breath you have to get rid of the VSC. Simply brushing your teeth won't do it. According to Dr. Barry Cash, a dentist at the Fresh Breath Center in Toronto, Canada, most patients should use a tongue scraper regularly to remove the debris that collects on the tongue, and apply a prescription gel to the tongue at night. The gel keeps the tongue oxygenated through the night and promotes the production of saliva.

EATING CELERY BURNS MORE CALORIES THAN ARE IN THE CELERY

HOW TRUE IS IT?
STICK TO THE FACTS—THIS ONE'S FALSE.

egative-calorie foods are the Holy Grail of dieters. Imagine a food that has so few calories that you burn up more just in the act of chewing and digesting it! Alas, imaginary is the right word for such a notion.

True, celery is very low in calories—there are about six calories in an eight-inch (20-centimeter) celery stalk. But by eating celery you are not kicking your body's calorie burner into overdrive. The Health and Fitness News Service reports that eating celery "burns only about the same number of calories as sitting and staring into space." This applies to the other miracle "negative-calorie" food, green bell peppers, and the fad diet of the mid-1990s, cabbage soup. So that's the downside of celery.

On the upside, celery is a good source of fiber. It is inexpensive and available in the supermarket all year round. And four ounces of raw celery—about three stalks—is rich in vitamin C and is a good source of potassium.

But the bottom line is, if you want to lose weight, you have to reduce your intake of calories, or find activities that will burn off more calories. The myth about negative-calorie foods is, according to Kelly Brownell, director of the Yale University Center for Eating Disorders, "just another sign of people looking for magic in weight loss."

CARRY A NEW BRIDE ACROSS THE THRESHOLD

HOW TRUE IS IT?
ONLY REASSURES THE
SUPERSTITIOUS.

*I*n parts of Mexico, the threshold of the bride's parents' house is the scene of an unusual drama. On the day of the wedding the bride pretends that she's had a change of heart. So the groom goes to the bride's house, where she waits just inside the threshold with her mother, her sisters, and her other female relatives. Once the groom arrives all the women make him sing, dance, and perform tricks before they agree that he is worthy after all and the marriage can go forward.

The oldest version of the threshold superstition goes back to ancient Rome. Just as a Mexican bride feigns to have lost interest in her groom, a newlywed Roman bride would refuse to cross the threshold of her new home to show that she was a modest, well-brought-up young woman reluctant to give up her virginity. She would only surrender her scruples after the groom lifted her up and carried her into the house.

The most widely known version of the threshold superstition comes from Scotland, where carrying the bride across the threshold of her new home was an early form of marriage insurance. Witches were said to place curses on the newlyweds' threshold to trip the bride as she crossed and thus kick off a lifetime of bad luck and marital misery. But the malevolence of the witch could be frustrated if the groom gallantly lifted his new wife across the doorsill and set her down safely inside the house.

The custom survives today as a quaint wedding tradition, although these days the groom is more likely to carry his bride across the threshold of the hotel room where they will spend

10 MOST COMMON WEDDING INSURANCE CLAIMS

1. Damage to wedding attire.

2. Photographs damaged or ruined.

3. Cancellation due to illness or bereavement in immediate family.

4. Caterer fails to turn up at the reception.

5. Lost wedding rings.

6. Wedding transport is a no-show.

7. Cancellation due to venue being double booked.

8. Property damage.

9. Lost or stolen wedding presents.

10. Supplier goes out of business.

(from E&L Insurance, United Kingdom)

the night before setting off on their honeymoon. But whatever its origin or modern equivalent, the old wives were just plain wrong about the threshold thing. Curses do not work, and demons and witches do not lurk at the entrance to houses, or apartments, or hotel rooms.

There are, however, plenty of real problems that can afflict a bride. And the way to ward off these disasters is appropriately modern: wedding insurance. Specialized insurance companies offer policies that will cover just about everything except the bride or groom changing her or his mind.

CARROTS ARE GOOD FOR THE EYES

HOW TRUE IS IT?
IF THEY COULD AFFORD
THEM, SOME RABBITS
MIGHT NEED GLASSES.

Some old wives believe that eating carrots is good for your eyesight in general. Other old wives insist that eating carrots provides a very specific benefit—namely, improved night vision.

Alas, both teams of old wives are a bit off the mark. Carrots do not sharpen your eyesight or boost your night vision. Carrots may, however, prevent macular degeneration, an eye disease that eventually leads to blindness. The secret ingredient is beta carotene that is present in spades in carrots (as well as in other vegetables such as squash, cabbage, spinach, and dandelion greens). In 1988, researchers at the University of Chicago studied 3,000 elderly Americans and found that something as simple as eating a single carrot a day reduced the risk of macular degeneration by as much as 40 percent.

Neil Bressler of the Johns Hopkins Medical Institutions in Baltimore, Maryland, came to the same conclusion regarding the positive effects of beta carotene. But Bressler found that for prevention of macular degeneration, beta carotene should be part of a program of vitamin supplements that includes vitamins C and E, zinc, and zinc oxide, all of which work to keep eyes healthy.

OSTRICHES BURY THEIR HEADS IN THE SAND

HOW TRUE IS IT?
IT JUST LOOKS THAT WAY.

*T*he old wives' tale that an ostrich, when it sees something dangerous or unpleasant coming, buries its head in the sand, is so popular that it's become a modern metaphor for someone who'd rather ignore a problem than face it head on. It's not true, but there is a bit of basis for the myth.

According to the World Wildlife Fund, an ostrich—especially an ostrich guarding a nest—will lie outstretched on the ground when it sees danger approaching. But this is a camouflage technique, not a case of the ostrich being in a state of denial. Furthermore, it is the job of the male ostrich to build a nest for forthcoming offspring, and he does this by using his bill to dig a shallow trench. Taken together, these two aspects of ostrich behavior account for the head-in-the-sand idea.

In real life, ostriches are anything but cowardly. They are aggressive with each other, giving one another short, hard pecks with their bills whenever they feel threatened, or if some other ostrich has invaded their turf. And there is something else that will set them off: ostrich farmers in Israel have found that a male and female ostrich must be of the same size if they are to mate. If two ostriches of different sizes are put in a pen together, they may try to hook up. But once they realize they can't get the job done, the ostriches attack each other.

IF YOU'RE CARRYING THE BABY HIGH, IT'S A GIRL

HOW TRUE IS IT?
ABOUT 50 PERCENT OF
THE TIME.

*T*he invention of ultrasound took a lot of steam out of the gender-guessing industry. Nonetheless, the old methods of gender divination still persist.

Where the mother is carrying her baby is said to be a surefire method of determining its gender. If you are carrying high, it's a girl. If you are carrying low, it's a boy. Doctors tell us, however, that the high/low thing is not a sign of the sex of the baby; rather, the shape of the mother's belly is an indication of her uterine and muscle tone combined with the baby's position. For example, the old wives will look at a woman who is carrying her baby low and say, "Ah ha! She's going to have a boy!" In fact, all that has happened is the baby has dropped lower into the pelvis because the mother is getting closer to delivery.

Then there is the basketball vs. watermelon theory. If a pregnant woman looks like she's carrying a perfectly round basketball, it's a boy. If she looks like she's carrying a wide watermelon, it's a girl. Statistically, that myth came out as a dead heat. You might as well toss a coin.

There are, of course, other traditional methods, all equally questionable. Mothers who can't get enough sweets will have a girl. Mothers who crave anything sour will have a boy. Some people say that breast size can reveal the baby's sex. If the mother's right breast is larger, she's having a boy. If her left breast is larger, she's having a girl.

Another rumored tell-tale sign is the physical condition of the father. If Dad starts putting on weight, his wife will have a girl.

NOT QUITE 50 PERCENT OF THE TIME

It is conventional to say that these pregnancy-related old wives' tales have a 50-50 chance of being correct. In fact, the odds are not so even. Globally, for every 100 girls born, between 104 and 107 boys are born. Recently in China the number has become much more skewed: in 2002, for every 100 girls, 116.9 boys were born. The preponderance of boys is an artificially created phenomenon thanks to the Chinese government's policy of one child per family. Many Chinese families prefer their only child to be a boy rather than a girl. A 1995 article in Hong Kong's *South China Morning Post* reported that it is not uncommon in China for women to abort a female fetus, or abandon a female infant and not report its birth, then try again in hopes of conceiving a boy.

The number of infants girls left at Chinese orphanages is so high that in 2002 Americans adopted 33,637 Chinese baby girls. Population experts predict that if this trend continues, by 2020 there will be 40 million more men than women in China.

If he doesn't gain any weight at all, she's having a boy. And then there's the original at-home pregnancy test. Take a gold pendant and hang it from a chain. Suspend the chain over the mother's belly. If the chain swings back and forth, it's a boy. If it moves in a circle, it's a girl.

MISTLETOE IS AN ANTIDOTE TO POISON

HOW TRUE IS IT?
THIS ONE'S PATENTLY
MISTLE-LEADING.

More than 2,000 years ago, the Celts of France and the British Isles believed that mistletoe was one of the most potent plants in the forest. Distilled in a liquid, or eaten fresh off the vine, mistletoe was thought to cure illness, boost fertility, and was just what the doctor ordered if you happened to have eaten something poisonous.

Nothing could be farther from the truth. Every part of the mistletoe is toxic. Eat just a few berries and your stomach will rebel. Eat many mistletoe berries and you could be in serious trouble. Mistletoe berries contain toxic proteins known as lectins; the leaves contain toxic amines. Both are lethal.

Although the medicinal reputation of mistletoe is a washout, it is a fascinating plant in many other respects. Mistletoe is a parasitic plant, which means it does not sprout out of the ground on its own. Rather, its sticky seeds—either windborne, or delivered via bird droppings—adhere to tree branches. From these seeds tiny roots burrow through the bark of the host until the roots reach the xylem, the inner tissue of the limb that conveys moisture and nutrients through the tree. Just as the xylem feeds the tree, it nourishes the mistletoe, too. A single mistletoe plant clinging to a healthy tree won't do much damage, but a tree that becomes the host to several mistletoe plants will die.

Because the Druids considered the plant an emblem of peace, delicate negotiations between warring Celtic tribes were held beneath the mistletoe. According to the rules, everyone present at the peace conference had to lay down his arms and maintain a truce for 24 hours. After the Celts were converted to Christianity, mistletoe survived as an emblem of friendship and goodwill.

The custom of kissing under the mistletoe developed from these earlier customs. Since mistletoe was associated with peace and goodwill, it seemed natural to bring it indoors at Christmas, the season of "peace on earth, goodwill to men." Usually the mistletoe was hung over the doorway, where guests were greeted with a friendly kiss. At some point during the 18th century in England, for reasons that are impossible to pin down, it became permissible for unmarried men to kiss any unmarried woman who happened to be standing under the mistletoe.

COOL FOODS ARE GOOD FOR A FEVER

HOW TRUE IS IT?
DON'T LET THEM FEED
YOU THIS LINE.

*I*n India, indeed in many parts of Asia, food tends to be divided into two large groups: cool and hot, and each of these types of food are appropriate for different circumstances.

During the sultry Asian summer, for example, Siong Mui Ng, the author of *Secrets of Nutritional Chinese Cooking*, suggests that you will be able to endure the heat and humidity better if you stay away from hot foods such as curry, red meat, anything fried, and chocolate. In place of beverages that stir up the blood, such as alcohol, you should drink chilled lime juice or iced lemon tea.

According to traditional Indian medicine, anyone suffering from a fever also should be fed only cool foods such as light soups, fish, yogurt drinks, and fruit. But will eating food that is cool or chilled actually diminish a fever? Yes, but only up to a point.

According to the doctors at North Shore General Pediatrics in New York, "Fever is the body's normal response to infections and helps to fight them off by turning on the body's immune system." The doctors explain that a fever is not an illness in itself, rather it is a symptom of an illness. There are ways to alleviate the symptom so the patient is more comfortable, but the fever won't go away entirely until the illness has been cured.

Eating cool foods may make the patient feel a bit better temporarily. But don't expect cool food to affect a cure. The immune system will do that by itself.

BLACK CATS BRING GOOD LUCK

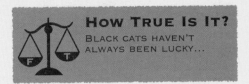

HOW TRUE IS IT?
BLACK CATS HAVEN'T
ALWAYS BEEN LUCKY...

*T*he old wives have concocted more myths about cats than possibly any other creature, particularly about whether they are lucky or unlucky. Opinion varies considerably depending on whereabouts in the world the old wives are. In the UK and Japan, black cats are considered symbols of good fortune, whereas in the US and Italy the opposite is true.

Some cultures traditionally consider black to be a protective color, particularly associated with fertility and prosperity. This manifests in traditions such as giving a bride a black cat as a wedding gift to ensure a happy marriage. Among fishing communities in northern England, a black cat in the home was considered to offer protection to the fishermen at sea.

In modern times, cats are bringing us all good fortune in another way. The Cat Genome Project, located at the National Cancer Institute in Maryland, is helping scientists gain insight into human disease. The domestic cat is considered to be a good animal model for human hereditary illnesses. More than 200 hereditable defects have been found in cats, many of which can be compared to human genetic defects.

The negative myths about black cats arose from their purported kinship with witches. Thousands of women in the 16th and 17th centuries were accused of practicing the dark arts, and black cats were killed in huge numbers along with their unfortunate owners. So if a black cat does cross your path, consider yourself lucky—we're all lucky that they survive to this day!

OPPOSITES ATTRACT

HOW TRUE IS IT?
THE OPPOSITE IS TRUE.

*T*wo people of wildly different backgrounds and interests meet and are smitten. Confronted with the depth and the intensity of their love, all conventional obstacles melt away. This is the basic plot of many myths, folk tales, novels, and movies. The supposed truism that opposites attract is so ingrained in our society that people who are brave enough to deride it out loud and in public are written off as cranks and cynics.

As is often the case, the cranks and the cynics got it right. For love—and even just for a roll in the hay—like seeks out like. Take a look at the data collected by the 1994 *Sex in America Survey*.

Let's start with race. Although today interracial couples find greater acceptance in American society than in years past, 94 percent of sexually active unmarried white men pair up with white women. In terms of other racial groups, 2.1 percent of white men have a Hispanic partner, 1.9 percent have an Asian partner, while only 0.6 percent have an African-American partner.

As for sexually active unmarried white women, 89.5 percent have a white partner, 6.4 percent have an African-American partner, 1.6 percent have a Hispanic partner, and only 0.7 percent have an Asian partner.

You can find the same pattern among African-Americans: 82 percent of black men choose a black woman as their partner, 7.6 percent have a white partner, and 4.6 percent have a Hispanic partner.

Among sexually active unmarried black women, 97 percent choose black men, while only 1 percent have a white partner and 1 percent an Asian partner.

The pattern holds true in other areas, too. For example, both men and women tend to have sex with partners who have their same level of education. The study found that 78 percent of men who never graduated high school only hooked up with women whose formal education stopped at high school.

Men who graduated from college also tended to look for love among other college graduates. Eight percent wandered farther afield by dating a woman with a graduate degree, but only 2 percent went to bed with a woman who had not finished high school. The rest enjoyed meetings of the mind.

Women were just as predictable: 81 percent of women who had no high school diploma paired up with men whose academic careers ended at high school. Seventy-one percent of women who had graduate degrees limited their field to men who had at least a bachelor's degree. None of the women with advanced degrees in the *Sex in America* sample slept with a man who had not finished high school.

Religious affiliation matters too. Even for premarital sex, 68 percent of Catholic men hook up with Catholic women. On the other side of the coin, the number is almost identical: 67 percent of Catholic women choose Catholic men. Among Protestant men, 61 percent pair up with Protestant women, and 72 percent of Protestant women choose Protestant men.

The study overturns the idea that we are not confined to the old ghettoes of race and class, religion and education. When we go hunting for a partner, our overwhelming tendency is to look for someone who reminds us a lot of ourselves.

LIARS CAN'T LOOK YOU IN THE EYE

HOW TRUE IS IT?
LOOK DEEP INTO MY EYES...

*Y*ou can't escape the scrutiny of the old wives; if you are not being honest with them, they will find you out because of your shifty eyes.

Or will they? Just how do you tell if someone is lying? In fact, numerous studies conducted since the 1970s show that the average person does no better than chance when they try to spot a person who is lying. You really need to know what to look for. San Francisco psychologist and researcher Paul Ekman believes the clue is in microexpressions. These are fleeting facial expressions that come and go in less than 40 milliseconds. They leak through even when someone is trying hard to conceal them, and most people never spot them. Specialist training programs, however, can improve people's skills in spotting these tiny clues, and the system has been used to train judges and police interrogators to enhance their investigative work.

Ekman's work has been built on by Mark Frank, a social psychologist at the University of Buffalo. Part of Frank's intention with his work is to debunk some of the common myths about how to read people. He says: "The literature shows that liars don't make less eye contact than truth tellers. But you ask anyone on the planet what liars do, the first thing they agree on is liars don't look you in the eye. Even just getting over that mythology is a step in the right direction."

USE THE FIVE-SECOND RULE
FOR DROPPED FOOD

HOW TRUE IS IT?
FIVE-SECOND RULES ARE
MADE TO BE BROKEN.

*I*t's known across the land as the "Five-Second Rule."
Any kind of food that hits the floor or the ground is still
safe to eat—provided you pick it up within five seconds.

If the Five-Second Rule sounds totally arbitrary, that's because it
is. During an internship at Professor Hans Blaschek's lab at the
University of Illinois during the summer of 2003, Jillian Clarke, an
enterprising 16-year-old student at the Chicago High School for
Agricultural Sciences, conducted a series of experiments to test
the veracity of the Five-Second Rule. She dropped candies and
cookies on ceramic tiles upon which she had brushed E. coli, a
type of bacteria found in raw meat and human feces, and one
that we run into just about everywhere every day.

After she had dropped the candies and the cookies on the
infected tiles, she studied them under an electron microscope.
Clarke found that E. coli stuck to the candy and the cookies
even if she snatched them up within the five seconds.

But there's more. Clarke did a demographic study of the Five-
Second Rule and discovered that:

1. 70 percent of women and 56 percent of men follow the Five-
   Second Rule.

2. People are more likely to pick up and eat cookies and candy.
   If the dropped food is a vegetable they don't use the Rule.

CHICKEN SOUP IS A GREAT FLU REMEDY

HOW TRUE IS IT?
IT'S NOT GOOD FOR THE CHICKEN, BUT IT'S GREAT FOR YOU.

*G*enerations have been nursed through colds and flu with a steaming bowl of chicken soup. The remedy is so strongly associated with Jewish grandmothers that chicken soup has been nicknamed "Jewish penicillin." In fact, it was a Jewish philosopher and physician, Moses Maimonides, who first recommended chicken soup for cold and flu sufferers back in the 12th century.

But is there anything to this long-standing tradition? You bet there is. Scientific literature across the globe agrees that chicken soup is packed with good stuff. As it simmers, chicken releases into the broth the amino acid cysteine, which, just like the drug acetylcysteine that is prescribed for bronchitis and other respiratory ailments, reduces the buildup of mucus and helps you breathe easier.

A study by the National University of Singapore went a step further. It found that chicken soup is not only good for colds, but is also good for a healthy heart. When laboratory rats that had been specifically bred to develop high blood pressure were fed mass-produced, over-the-counter chicken stock (not even homemade!), researchers found that, over the course of a year, the rats' heart swelling was reduced by around 40 to 50 percent, and the thickening of their blood vessels was reduced by 60 percent.

The Singapore scientists believe the secret ingredient is a type of protein known as a peptide. Just about all meat contains peptides, yet only peptide from chickens made human blood vessels healthier. Peptides from other meats, such as pork or beef, were also tested, but they had no effect. The researchers still are not sure why chicken peptide works when others do not.

One of the most interesting studies of the chicken soup phenomenon was conducted by Stephen Rennard, M.D., chief of pulmonary medicine at the University of Nebraska Medical Center in Omaha. He tested the chicken soup recipe handed down to his wife from her Lithuanian grandmother. Dr. Rennard found that chicken soup has anti-inflammatory properties.

Coughing and congestion, two common symptoms of colds and flu, are the result of inflammation produced by white blood cells known as neutrophils that pile up in the bronchial tubes. In the lab Dr. Rennard found that chicken soup diminished the ability of neutrophils to accumulate. Chicken soup proved so potent that even when it had been diluted 200 times it was still a good neutrophil inhibitor.

And there's more: although Dr. Rennard's grandmother-in-law's recipe does not call for it, you can boost your chicken soup's antiviral and antibacterial properties by adding garlic.

And don't leave out the pepper—it contains capsaicin, which works like cough medicine, suppressing coughs and reducing mucus. Even the heat of the soup helps loosen congestion, while the broth helps to keep you hydrated—absolutely essential for all cold and flu sufferers.

Of course, some cold sufferers have no talent in the kitchen. For them, Dr. Rennard also tested commercial chicken soup and found still more good news: canned chicken soup can be just as effective as homemade. Although it doesn't taste as good as Grandma's.

FISH IS BRAIN FOOD

*B*ertie Wooster, the barely averagely astute hero of countless *Jeeves and Wooster* stories by P.G. Wodehouse, always believed that his valet Jeeves must have consumed fish by the barrelful. What else could account for Jeeves's prodigious ability to get Bertie and his feckless pals out of one fearsome scrape after another?

It turns out that on the subject of seafood's ability to stimulate the little gray cells, Bertie was right on the money. Scientists suspected as much back in the 19th century, although those early proponents of the fish-is-brain-food school of nutrition mistakenly believed it was the phosphorus in fish that did the job. Today, researchers believe a fatty compound known as docosahexaenoic acid (DHA) is the stuff that makes the brain work harder and better. In fact, DHA is the fundamental building block of brain tissue. The more DHA the body takes in through diet, the more fuel the brain has to work with. On the other hand, a diet low in DHA could translate into deficient brain function.

Some medical studies have found evidence that people who eat a lot of seafood (and consequently have high levels of DHA) are less susceptible to depression. A report published in the *American Journal of Clinical Nutrition* found that in fish-eating nations such as Japan and Korea, the incidence of depression among the populace tends to be low. At the opposite end of the spectrum, in nations such as the United States and Canada, where fish is eaten rarely, DHA levels are low, and depression rates are high.

In a separate study, researchers in the Netherlands found that elderly men who ate a lot of fish were less likely than their meat-eating neighbors to suffer from memory loss. Meanwhile, in Japan, researchers reported improved short-term memory among patients who received DHA supplements.

The University of Texas Medical Branch in Galveston studied the impact of fish on memory from a different angle. High levels of zinc are found in fish. The Texas team found that memory declines in individuals whose diet does not include much zinc. When participants in the Texas study started eating higher levels of zinc-rich foods, such as fish, their verbal recall skills increased 12 percent and their ability to remember visual patterns jumped 17 percent. Researchers at England's University of Surrey teamed up with their colleagues at Purdue University in Indiana and discovered links between low levels of DHA and such disorders as dyslexia, attention deficit disorder, and hyperactivity.

After studying DHA levels in children, Professor Michael Crawford, director of London's Institute of Brain Chemistry and Human Nutrition, reported that schoolkids with the highest levels of DHA behaved better and outperformed their classmates who showed low levels of DHA. Professor Crawford has gone on the record to encourage pregnant women to eat a lot of fish such as salmon, pollock and shrimp, arguing that the brainiac benefits of DHA in the mother's body will be passed along to her unborn child.

Coldwater fish, particularly salmon, tuna, mackerel, and herring, have the highest levels of DHA. Just eating a few seafood meals a week can help to boost your DHA level. A word of caution, however: pregnant women should avoid fish that tend to have high levels of mercury. These include tuna, mackerel, shark, swordfish, snapper, orange roughy, marlin, and grouper.

SOME LOTTERY NUMBERS COME UP AGAIN AND AGAIN

HOW TRUE IS IT?
THE ODDS ARE AGAINST IT.

*I*f experience teaches us anything, it is that working hard gets us nowhere. The best way to hit the Big Score is to win the lottery. According to the old wives, there are certain winning numbers that appear time and again in the lottery.

And the old wives are right! For example, between January 1989 and June 2005, some numbers have been drawn more than others. The number 34 was the most frequently drawn, appearing 271 times (the choices range from 1 to 42). Number 9 has been a winning number 252 times, 10 has been drawn 249 times, 30 has come up 248 times, 12 has been among the winning numbers 247 times, followed closely by the numbers 2 and 17, which have been drawn 245 times.

Knowing which numbers turn up most often is useful, but how often do all six winning numbers repeat themselves? According to Colorado Lottery statisticians, the same six winning numbers will recur every 2,700 drawings. Before you get excited, consider that Colorado holds only 104 drawings every year, so you'll have to wait 16 or 17 years before the winning six come back again.

English statisticians caused quite a stir when their findings indicated England's National Lottery might not be random. In their 2002 report entitled *The Randomness of the National Lottery*, Dr. John Haigh and Professor Charles Goldie, both members of the Royal Statistical Society, found that number 38 popped up among the winning numbers most often: in 637 games played between 1994 and 2002, lucky 38 was drawn 107 times. But in the December 16, 2004 issue of the English newspaper *The Guardian*, journalist David Adams offered readers the following advice: "Don't put your house on it."

The 2002 report "may have suggested the number 38 ball be 'physically examined' because it was sucked out of the machine so often, but the 100 or so draws since have seen it fall back into the statistically normal pack. Plus, if there was a physical anomaly with the ball, it would have to be repeated in each of the eight possible sets used for the main Lotto draw, of which one is selected at random each week." Haigh and Goldie's findings were, according to Adams, "a freak." But England's National Lottery Commission took them seriously enough to ask the University of Salford's Centre for the Study of Gambling for a second opinion. "All tests support the hypothesis of randomness," this think tank concluded. "That is, they confirm no evidence of nonrandomness among the Lotto draws."

Before you rush off and buy a pile of tickets, however, bear in mind that these results are based on anecdotal evidence. As Stephen Jay Gould writes in *Streak: Joe DiMaggio and the Summer of '41*, "The statistics of streaks and slumps"—or in our case, allegedly lucky numbers—"do teach an important lesson…about life in general. The history of a species, or any natural phenomenon that requires unbroken continuity in a world of trouble, works like a batting streak. All are games of a gambler playing with a limited stake against a house with infinite resources. The gambler must eventually go bust. His aim can only be to stick around as long as possible, to have some fun while he's at it, and, if he happens to be a moral agent as well, to worry about staying the course with honor."

The sobering truth is, every number has an equal chance of being selected on any given day. There is no magic formula for winning the lottery.

NO TWO SNOWFLAKES
ARE EXACTLY ALIKE

HOW TRUE IS IT?
THIS ONE'S NO JOKE.

*H*ow could it be that every single individual snowflake would be one of a kind? In his explanation, Kenneth G. Libbrecht of Caltech starts with electrons. According to Libbrecht, particle physics tells us that because electrons have no component parts—in other words, they aren't made up of other things—one electron looks exactly like every other electron.

A snowflake, or snow crystal, as Libbrecht calls them, is made up of about 10 quintillion water molecules (a quintillion is a 1 followed by 18 zeros). In order for two snow crystals to be exactly alike, all those water molecules would have to arrange themselves in precisely the same positions. But they don't, and not just because there are 10 quintillion parts to deal with. As the water molecules float from the clouds through the sky toward the ground, they are affected by changes in the temperature, the amount of moisture in the air, and collisions with the microscopic bits of ash and dust that fill Earth's atmosphere. As the snow crystal makes it way through this obstacle course, it assumes a random, complex, and very beautiful pattern.

Given the 10 quintillion water molecules and the unpredictable impediments the snow crystal encounters, Professor Libbrecht assures us, "the probability of two crystals growing with exactly the same pattern of dislocations is vanishingly small."